Strategic Workforce Planning

Guidance & Back-up Plans

Tracey Smith,
BMath, MASc, MBA

ABOUT THE AUTHOR

Tracey Smith led the global strategic workforce planning initiative for FedEx Express World Headquarters. In addition, she led a variety of global, strategic HR projects where expertise in data-driven decision making was required. She is now an independent consultant advising clients on HR analytics and workforce planning.

Tracey holds a BMath degree in Applied Mathematics and a MASc degree in Mechanical Engineering from the University of Waterloo, Canada specializing in numerical modeling. She also holds an MBA from Texas Christian University specializing in forecasting, operational analysis and supply chain.

Tracey provides a wide variety of strategic and analytical services and has over 25 years of experience in the areas of Human Resources, Supply Chain and Engineering. Her clients are primarily located in Canada and the U.S. Her company, Numerical Insights LLC, helps clients make better business decisions by utilizing data-driven techniques. These techniques focus effort on business decisions which will yield the most value or reduce risk.

Tracey presents on a variety of business topics at conferences and seminars, primarily on the strategic benefits of data analysis and its value to the organization. Her presentations combine strategic theory with real-world implementation.

Tracey is the author of multiple books which can be found on her website, www.numericalinsights.com, in the Appendix of this book and on Amazon book sites worldwide. Tracey has been recognized as one of the HR Analytics experts to follow in 2017 and 2018.

Never let the future disturb you. You will meet it, if you have to, with the same weapons of reason which today arm you against the present.

Marcus Aurelius

CONTENTS

ABOUT THE AUTHOR..iii

1 Introduction 1

How to Navigate this Book..1

What is Strategic Workforce Planning? 2

The Evolution 4

The Purpose of Strategic Workforce Planning................................7

How Will This Help My Company? 7

Where Are We Now? 9

2. The Strategic Workforce Planning Framework 13

The Role of Business Strategy 18

Step 1: Determine the Roles of Interest 21

Step 2: Establish the Current State 38

Step 3: Determine Desired Forecasting Scenarios.......................41

Step 4: Perform Gap Assessments 51

Step 5: Establish Action Plans 57

Environmental Scanning 60

3. Implementation 64

Selling the Concept 65

Challenges to Successful Implementation 70

Implementation Planning...76

When Selling the Concept Just Didn't Work 80

Measuring Success 81

Roles and Responsibilities..86

Workforce Planning's Connection to HR Activities 93

4. Baby Boomers and the Risk to Your Leadership 96

5. Concluding Remarks 102

Numerical Insights on the Web.. 104

Appendix A: Tools and Templates 105

Step 1: Determine Roles of Interest.. 105

Step 2: Establishing the Current State 106

Step 3: Determine Desired Forecasting Scenarios.............................. 107

Step 4: Perform Gap Assessments 108

Environmental Scanning Reference 109

Appendix B: Other Publications by the Author 110

Bibliography 112

1 Introduction

How to Navigate this Book

The material in this book is organized such that it provides the following information in order:

- an overview of strategic workforce planning and how it evolved,
- a detailed description of each step in the author's framework for strategic workforce planning, and
- practical tools and advice for those responsible for implementing this process.

Those who are new to strategic workforce planning should start reading at the beginning. Those with a bit more experience should be able to read through the detailed steps of the framework and select the pieces that would provide added value to the reader's specific organization.

While this book will provide information on all stages of the strategic workforce planning process, I want to stress to readers that it is absolutely possible to derive a great deal of value from individual planning activities without having implemented a fully integrated program. Additionally, this value can be obtained with virtually no budget.

What is Strategic Workforce Planning?

The dynamics of a global economy and the rapid pace at which it changes have made strategic workforce planning (SWP) one of the "most sought after skills in HR today." For the Fortune 100, this topic has received an increased executive focus as companies attempt to mitigate workforce risk in an uncertain economy and deal with the "challenges of change."

There are many statistics supporting the urgency of SWP. One of the most insightful is the fact that "60% of the jobs in the 21st century require skills possessed by 20% of the workforce." Additionally, a report issued by the World Economic Forum, "Towards a Reskilling Revolution," concluded that "95% of the 1.4 million US workers who are expected to be displaced in the next decade can be transitioned to new positions with similar skills and higher wages." They urgency now is in retraining those workers.

Currently, strategic workforce planning in the corporate world is looking at supply, demand and the quantitative gap between them. The ability to judge the readiness of employees and the ability to project changing competency needs is in its infancy. With changes occurring as quickly as they are today, strategic workforce planning becomes even more essential.

Strategic workforce planning is a proactive approach which plans to provide:

- the right number of people,
- with the right skill sets,
- in the right location,
- at the right time,
- at the right cost

to ensure successful completion of business objectives. In some definitions you may see the first two bullets captured as "the right people" but I like to clarify that the right people actually means the right number with the right skills.

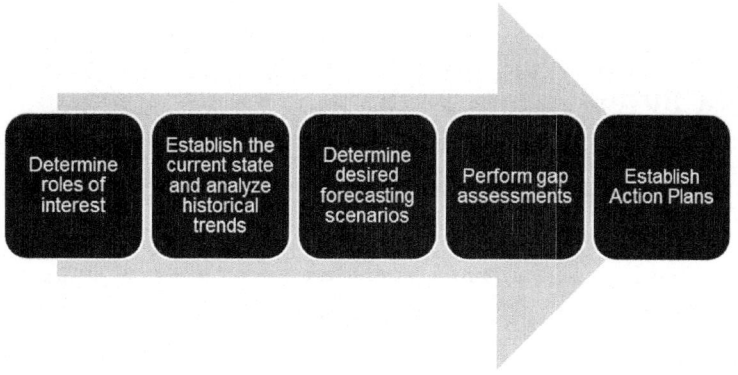

Figure 1: Strategic Workforce Planning Framework

The five major steps in the **Strategic workforce planning framework** are:

- Determine the roles of interest
- Establish the current state and historical trends
- Determine desired forecasting scenarios
- Perform gap assessments (in headcount and skill sets)
- Establish action plans

Strategic workforce planning is the central activity unifying and guiding the strategic direction of many human resource functions. It can:

- assess overall human capital risk for the organization,
- assess the risk of your employee supply,
- assess the risk of employee demand,
- assess the gap between supply and demand,
- determine talent management development needs through competency analysis, and
- set the direction for recruitment needs and priorities.

The Evolution

Like most business processes, evolution will occur as knowledge grows and technology increases. In my previous guide book on data driven decision making (Appendix B), I presented the evolution of data analysis capabilities within an organization. The evolution of workforce planning follows a similar path.

The evolution has four main stages and begins with simple headcount planning. In this stage, companies base their workforce analysis on internal factors only and assume that they exist in a stable environment. It doesn't take much contemplation in modern day to realize we exist in a world of instability, so I do not recommend leaving your company in this stage. Basing business decisions on an assumption of stability will expose your business to a larger amount of risk. The forward looking time span in this stage is usually very short and there is no linkage to the business strategy. Some workforce planners reference this stage as manpower planning.

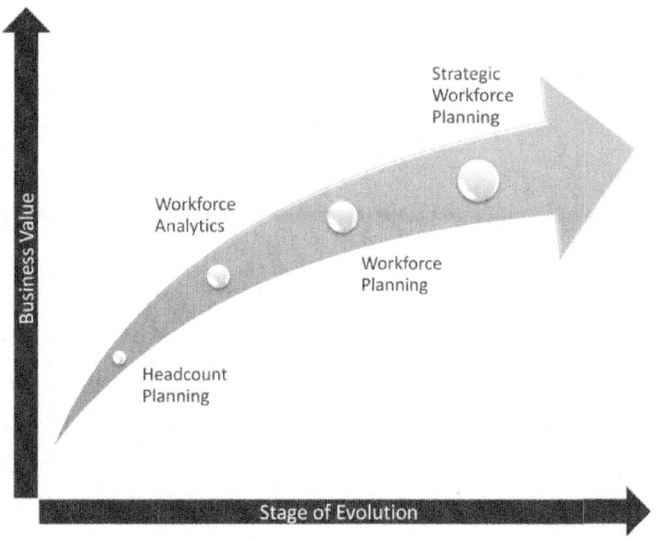

Figure 2: The Evolution of Workforce Planning

The second stage of evolution is that of workforce analytics. This stage is more quantitative than its predecessor. Instead of looking at a very brief timeline, this stage begins to look at trend analysis. The data examined is longer term and the focus is on both the present and the past. Much of the reported analytics in this stage are the familiar measures of turnover, engagement and performance appraisal scores with the goal of determining whether they are trending upward or downward. These trends would set the expectations for the near future and negative trends would initiate remedial actions in the Human Resources department. This stage is characterized by the use of dashboards to display the trending information. Like the first stage, this stage also has no linkage to the business strategy.

The third stage is workforce planning. This is where both internal trends and external factors are considered in terms of their impact on labour, but the process is still disconnected from the business strategy. This is the stage which takes into consideration external information whereas previous stages rely on internal information only.

The final stage of workforce planning evolution is strategic workforce planning. This is where the connection to the business strategy finally takes place. The business strategy drives the business objectives and the business plan. These plans are forward looking and in most companies are three to five year plans. How far out a company projects its plan is a function of items like industry maturity, growth, the amount of instability in the market and risk levels associated with potentially disruptive technologies.

Strategic workforce planning segments out the roles which have the greatest impact on the successful execution of the business objectives and concentrates workforce planning efforts on these roles. The aim is to protect and develop those skills within the organization to ensure a pipeline of these skills for the future. The amount of attention required to manage these roles makes it inconceivable to dedicate resources to managing every role. There is no business case for this. That's not to say that non-strategic roles are ignored, but rather they fall in line with receiving a standard level of attention from HR much like one would dedicate more attention to a company's best customers rather than on a large number of small ones.

The Purpose of Strategic Workforce Planning

Strategic workforce planning is about defining the workforce that can execute the organization's strategy, now and in the future. It answers questions such as:

- What are the impacts of demographic shifts and external factors? External factors can include market trends, technology changes, new competency needs, social changes etc.
- What new roles and competencies are needed in the workforce today and in the future?
- What is the gap between supply and demand of talent?
- How can we ensure that the right people are in the right jobs with the right skills at the right time for the right cost?
- Do we build or buy talent to meet our needs?
- Can our planning react quickly enough when conditions change?
- Knowing all of the above, what actions are needed to fulfill the strategic workforce planning goals in order to support the organization's strategy?

How Will This Help My Company?

Studies suggest that as much as 80% of most organization's assets are intangible and company valuations are increasingly based on human capital. As such, the benefits of strategic workforce planning are far-reaching.

Strategic workforce planning adds strategic value by turning business strategy into action. It drives talent practices both now and in the future. To turn strategy into action, it is necessary to determine the "business critical" roles that drive strategic achievement.

Strategic workforce planning also mitigates risk. Tools like scenario planning can help a company prepare for a variety of possible futures and can help determine the amount of flexibility needed for the future. Assessments combining information on both the supply and demand of the workforce can identify hidden risks or eliminate unsubstantiated risks.

If done correctly, strategic workforce planning can drive efficiencies and ROI. Companies have used strategic workforce planning forecasting to predict not only their talent needs but also their property needs, their new employee IT requirements, training needs, budgets and more.

As an example, one company with office space constraints determined several job categories which did not require an office. Their forecast determined how many offices they needed (and did not need). It determined how many new computers they needed and to which locations these should be deployed. Additionally, it determined the quantities and types of new employee training.

While many companies have concerns over these remote working arrangements, studies have shown in several companies that these employees were more productive because they value the "perk" of not having to commute. In fact, studies have shown that these workers provide additional hours of work for their employer since they tend to work through the time they normally would have spent commuting. These companies benefit from higher employee productivity, savings from not having to lease another office location, better employee retention, greater flexibility in locating its employees and better response time from IT and training for new employees.

Strategic workforce planning can help ensure that replacements are available to fill important vacancies. It can further provide realistic staffing projections for budgeting purposes and help prepare for restructuring, reducing or expanding a workforce to keep up with change.

Additional uses of strategic workforce planning include:

- to forecast the cost of future retirements,
- to investigate a natural attrition solution as an alternative to down-sizing actions,
- to protect specialized talent,
- to assess the risk to the continuity of leadership, and
- to assess the true mobility of your workforce.

As far-reaching as the strategic workforce planning applications are, the key to successful implementation is <u>the ability to derive action plans from these analyses</u>. Since the majority of these actions are related to HR functions (talent management, recruitment, training, redeployment of staff), the strategic workforce planning function most frequently resides in HR. HR serves as the liaison coordinating the linkages between the business customers (Finance, Operations, etc.), the business strategy owners, the company economist and the various HR sub-teams.

Where Are We Now?

In 2008, a survey concluded that two thirds of U.S. employers have no planning for their future talent needs (Capelli, 2008). Also in 2008, a global survey by Top Grade found that companies were "not very prepared to address many of the global workforce trends" (Gross, 2008) but many organizations had made changes to their Human Resource programs as a result of investigating the benefits of strategic workforce planning.

Around the same time, IBM reported that only 13% of organizations felt that they were good at predicting skills needed in the future. This is one of the more challenging skills, especially in times of rapidly changing technology.

By 2009, i4cp reported that 70% of companies surveyed indicated that workforce planning initiatives were growing. The same survey, conducted again in 2011, reported that 76% of companies indicated that workforce planning activities were underway. Keeping in mind that this survey was conducted on i4cp's clients who are primarily the Fortune 500, the value presented would likely be much smaller when we consider a broader field of organizations.

The 2011 i4cp (i4cp, 2012) survey also reported that, "higher-performing organizations, based on five-year performance in revenue growth, profitability, customer satisfaction and market share, engage in workforce planning activities to a much greater extent than lower-performers. However, the greatest growth in workforce planning is occurring in lower-performing organizations."

By 2012, many of the Fortune 500 have investigated the benefits of workforce planning and have presented frameworks for it to their leadership. Additionally, the first conferences arose which were dedicated entirely to this topic and research firms had created a service to coordinate exchanges (groups) with their clients in order to provide a forum through which best practices are shared.

Today, the state of workforce planning remains in its infancy in many organizations and those leading the workforce planning function have realized that it is a journey of several years both in execution and leadership adoption. With that, come several challenges, many of which will be discussed in the section *Challenges to Successful Implementation*.

Additionally, the same survey by i4cp suggests that 50% of companies surveyed consider their workforce planning efforts to be operational and 20% consider their efforts to be tactical. Only 20% of respondents felt that their workforce efforts were strategic.

In July 2012, a controversial issue arose when the Society for Human Resource Management (SHRM) proposed the standardization of human capital metrics. If standardized, these metrics would be guided by the American National Standards Institute (ANSI) and there would be a template used for companies to report their human capital information to shareholders. This effort began back in 2009 when ANSI designated SHRM as a standards developing organization.

While SHRM and the companies who helped form these standards try to gain support, the proposal has been met with a large amount of resistance (Fister, 2012). An article in May 2012 by i4cp outlined views that SHRM was over-reaching in trying to show its value to investors and that it should first prove the impact to the bottom line.

The HR Policy Association (HRPA), whose membership includes senior leaders of more than 300 large U.S. companies, agreed that putting these standards in place would further burden public companies who are already dedicating large amounts of resources to Sarbanes-Oxley (Metrics, Schmetrics, 2012).

Working with a large, global Fortune 100, I tend to agree with those who oppose the standard. Regardless of the extra resources required to do this reporting, when it comes to human capital analytics, it would not be possible to gain agreement on how to report the analytics in the same way for each company. It was a large undertaking in one Fortune 100 to get five global regions to agree on a small series of HR metric definitions. I can't imagine an entire standard. As such, trying to compare across companies wouldn't hold much value for investors.

Additionally, as an analytical person, I agree that SRHM needs to prove the impact to the bottom line before we commit resources to this task.

2. The Strategic Workforce Planning Framework

If you are looking for the one, official framework representing the steps of strategic workforce planning, there isn't one. There are almost as many frameworks as there are companies doing strategic workforce planning. A quick internet search will reveal the five steps presented on Wikipedia, the seven steps presented by IBM, the seven step process by i4cp and the eight steps presented by the Human Capital Institute. Additionally, I developed my own framework for the Fortune 100 which employs me so that it would align with a way of thinking familiar to management and be easily understood.

The most complicated framework I have ever seen was one presented by a large consulting company. I often wonder whether the complexity of the framework graphic was an intentional move designed to deter companies from doing their own workforce planning.

The frameworks for workforce planning can be very simple. The complexity is added when you try to execute each of the steps within the existing framework of your business. It is for this reason that so many frameworks exist since we all operate under different internal processes.

Since strategic workforce planning relies on many linkages to internal processes in order to succeed, the strategic workforce planning function cannot operate in isolation. If it did, we could all use the same framework.

To provide a few examples of frameworks, Wikipedia outlines five steps:

1. Environmental Scan
2. Current Workforce Profile
3. Future Workforce View
4. Analysis and Targeted Future
5. Closing the gaps

If you were new to workforce planning, the Wikipedia description would certainly be confusing since it gives no hint that you need to segment the workforce before conducting these steps. Otherwise, you will waste valuable resources evaluating positions that are of little consequence to business success.

As a second example, the i4cp web site presents a seven step framework as shown below. I find the second label, "Human Capital Mapping" to be unclear at first glance and I haven't seen it used in other frameworks.

The framework presented by the Human Capital Institute (HCI) is clearer. This framework demonstrates that the process should be iterative with your business strategy, i.e., the cycle repeats over time and business plans are updated each year.

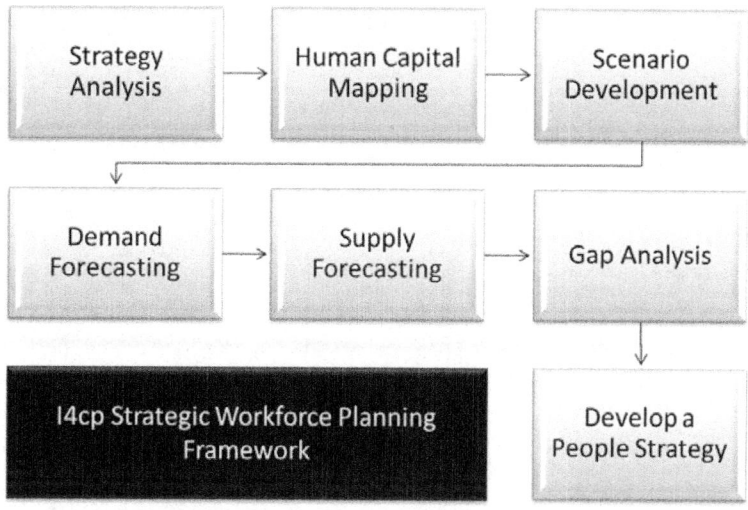

Figure 3: i4cp Seven Steps to Strategic Workforce Planning

The one step which may confuse newcomers to workforce planning is the environmental scan. In HCI's model, an internal and external scan of the environment is included. The external scan examines items like economic conditions, competitive threats and industry trends. The internal scan examines the company strategy, business goals, technology changes and employee profile data.

From the author's point of view, this framework is a good guideline but needs to be modified for many organizations. For my own Fortune 100 company, many of the environmental scan activities would have been performed in the formation of the business strategy and 5-year plan. I will provide an expanded explanation of environmental scanning near the end of this chapter.

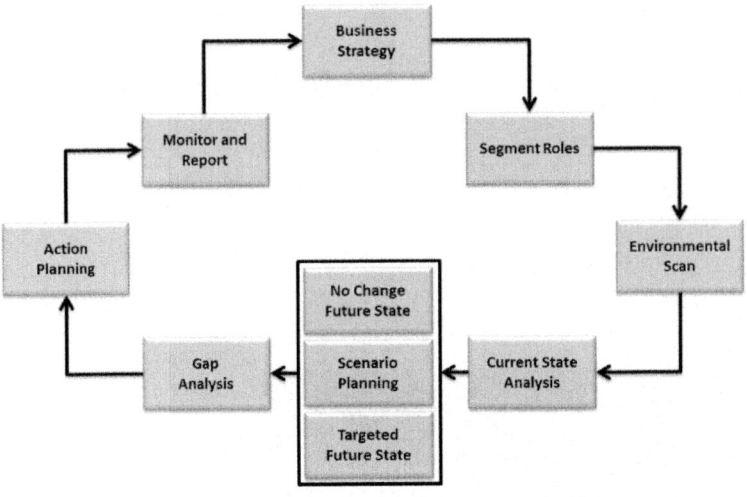

Figure 4: Human Capital Institute Framework

As a final example, I will present the framework I developed for my own use (Figure 5: Author's Strategic Workforce Planning Framework). I will begin with a high level description and then present the specific activities for each of the five steps throughout this chapter. The goal in developing this framework was to keep it as simple as possible for ease of communication to the company's leadership and employees.

The leadership of large organizations is bombarded with many business cases trying to obtain support for a variety of initiatives. Having compared practices with dozens of large organizations, one of the common challenges for workforce planning leaders is in obtaining this support and the associated funding. Recommendations related to this challenge will be discussed in Chapter 3.

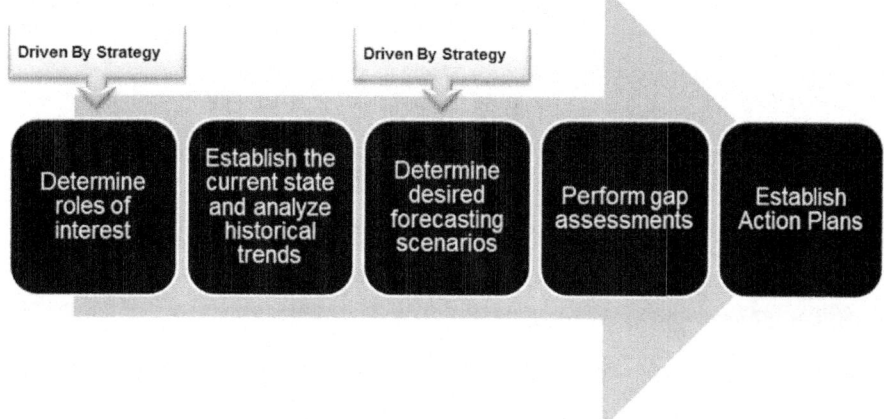

Figure 5: Author's Strategic Workforce Planning Framework

In a paper issued by i4cp (Morrison, 2012), the overwhelming answer to the top challenge facing business leaders for strategic workforce planning was a lack of resources. The remaining challenges rounding out the top five were: technologies that do not share data effectively, a rapidly changing business environment, a lack of workforce planning know-how and ineffective communication across business functions.

Additional confusion has been found within Human Resource groups where employees confuse talent management with workforce planning. As I explain the details behind my framework, you will clearly see the division between the two and where they intersect.

What we notice when we compare these frameworks is that each contains the same fundamental steps, although some of the steps are in a different order and others head into a more detailed division of steps.

The three core steps in all of these frameworks are:

1. Take a look at the current state.
2. Try to forecast the future state.
3. Try to close the gap between the future and today.

One important point to make is that strategic workforce planning cannot be done without the connection to the business strategy. The frameworks which do not demonstrate this connection run the risk of strategic workforce planning being interpreted as a stand-alone function.

You will probably notice that the three core steps shown above are very similar to the steps of continuous improvement. Since strategic workforce planning is a cyclical process, i.e. we revisit our workforce analyses periodically, it is actually a method to continuously improve the workforce in order to meet the changing needs of the business. These changing needs could be the result of changes in the industry, changes in technology, changes in necessary skill sets and changes in economic conditions.

Using the framework I presented in Figure 5, let's take a look at some of the components.

The Role of Business Strategy

As mentioned above, strategic workforce planning must be driven by the business strategy. It cannot succeed in isolation. However, that's not to say that you can't put some portion of the workforce planning process in place while establishing the link to the business strategy, especially if you find yourself implementing workforce planning from the bottom up. I will discuss this more in the section on implementing workforce planning in the *Challenges to Successful Implementation* section in Chapter 3.

Workforce planning should begin with a clear statement of the business strategy. The business strategy generates the business plan which in most

companies is a 3-5 year outlook. This business strategy takes into account items such as the forecasted economic conditions, the impact of possible political uncertainties and elections, market and industry conditions, changing technologies and possible changes in regulations. Health care changes in the U.S. are a good example of regulatory changes impacting organizations. Economic instability in Europe and slowing growth in China are certainly economic conditions affecting virtually all businesses.

The strategic workforce planning lead in an organization should have a seat at the table when the business plan is discussed and finalized. Their participation level will vary based on their overall business expertise and how well HR has been integrated into the company. At a minimum, HR should be in the room in order to start thinking about the impacts the strategy will have on the workforce. The key thing to remember here is that strategic workforce planning is the process which takes the business strategy and derives the people strategy.

Looking at the workforce planning framework presented in Figure 5, there are two main steps where the business strategy drives the workforce planning activities. This is why I cannot stress enough the importance of establishing a connection to the business strategy as one of the first steps in implementing workforce planning.

In the first step of the framework, we determine the roles of interest. The business strategy determines which roles within the organization are critical to the successful execution of the strategy and critical to the organization's future. I will discuss this step in more detail shortly.

In Step 3 of the framework, the business strategy is what determines the desired forecasting scenarios. Recall that the strategy development included all of the environmental considerations (business environment) in order to create the list of "possible futures."

How does knowledge of the business strategy then translate into the people strategy? The strategic workforce planning framework steps will guide you there. Here is one example. Knowing how your company makes money will guide you to the jobs that are most crucial in generating revenue. This would be discovered in the role segmentation step. Knowing these positions, is there a good pipeline of candidates for these jobs? This pipeline can be internal or external. Recognizing that this pipeline is important to the future of the business, your people plans may include talent development plans, training plans and recruitment plans to maintain this pipeline.

Let's take a look at another example. What are the key business objectives for your company for the next 5 years? Is there a large shift in skill sets needed for your future? If so, can you develop these new competencies in your existing workforce or do you need to locate external candidates? If you develop the skills in-house, will that leave vacancies in the employee base as you migrate the employees into this new role? If you can't develop your current employees into this new role, is there a group of employees who become obsolete? The answer to all of these questions will drive the specific actions in your people plans.

As a final comment on the importance of linking strategic workforce planning to the business strategy, without knowledge of the strategic plans for the coming years, the strategic workforce planning function would simply be a function predicting the future workforce under the assumption that past conditions will continue into the future. I call this the "steady as she goes" scenario. Recalling the stages of evolution in Chapter 1, this would be workforce analytics and not strategic workforce planning.

Now that we've covered the role that business strategy plays in the strategic workforce planning process, let's take a look at the specific steps.

Step 1: Determine the Roles of Interest

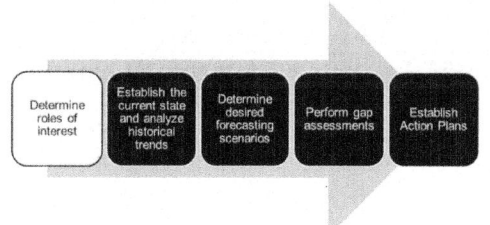

The roles of interest in an organization are the ones required to successfully accomplish the strategic objectives. Strategic objectives are defined by the business strategy. Looking at the roles in an organization, why do we begin workforce planning by segmenting the roles or determining roles of interest?

For most companies, there would be little value in dedicating strategic workforce planning resources to analyzing roles that are not critical or pivotal to your company. Therefore this step is designed to focus the efforts of the strategic workforce planning staff on roles that matter the most and where changes to those roles yield the most value. It should be noted that the assessment in this step is of the *roles* and not the *people* in the roles.

Why do I say "determine the roles of interest" when the more popular convention is to say "determine the critical or pivotal roles?" The answer to this question is related to corporate culture. If your company operates in silos (as many large companies do), there is a tendency for the leaders of each silo to view his / her area as the most important and to view the majority of roles within his / her organization as critical. In fact, in one large company, an attempt several years ago to define the critical roles at the leadership levels resulted in all but one position being classified as critical.

There can also be a certain ego factor involved when you propose that certain roles are not critical to the organization. By communicating that you are seeking the "roles of interest," it is easier to explain that the roles you seek are those that are closely tied to the execution of the business strategy and 3-5 year plan. Referencing roles as critical and non-critical, especially in difficult financial times, makes employees in the non-critical roles very nervous. Using the phrase "roles of interest" can actually make those employees feel safer just by the fact that no one is looking too closely at them.

So, how do we proceed with determining the roles of interest? There are a variety of thought processes and tools which have been presented in the literature and at numerous conferences. Let's take a look at several approaches and determine the strengths of each one.

One method, presented by the Cornell University School of Industrial and Labor Relations (Snell), is to form a two by two matrix where one axis ranks how strongly the position contributes to the success of the business and the other axis ranks the level of difficulty in acquiring those skills in the market.

Let's look at two types of roles in the Human Resources function to see how this could work. Within most Human Resource functions, the employees are one of two kinds. Some employees serve their internal customers by performing day-to-day tactical activities like processing new hires and answering questions about policies and benefits. On the other extreme are the strategic HR employees who are leading projects which support the business strategy, assessing competency needs for the future and implementing leadership development activities.

Considering the activities required in these roles, the tactical HR employee would be less important to the business since they perform fairly routine activities and they are not linked to the business strategy.

Additionally, because the skill sets required to perform tactical HR activities are not highly advanced, it should be fairly easy to find these skill sets in the market. Therefore, people in a tactical HR role would be placed in the bottom-left quadrant on the matrix.

Keep in mind that even in the tactical HR roles, there will be substantial variation in the placement positon in this matrix. While recruiters may be easy to find in the market, you may have other tactical HR roles which are more difficult to fill. Consider for example, a company which needs its HR reps to be familiar with labour regulations in multiple countries instead of only one. This skill set combination will be harder to locate which would shift the role placement further up the matrix and to the right.

On the other hand, employees in a strategic HR role are usually required to have a higher level of education and experience. Their roles usually involve projects that are closely tied to the people strategy of the company which should be directly tied to the business strategy.

Additionally, because of the level of education and experience required, people with these skill sets are not as easy to obtain as the tactical HR skill sets. Therefore, people in the strategic HR roles would be placed in the upper-right quadrant of the matrix.

In the interest of simplicity, I have only considered a few factors in determining the level of difficulty in obtaining talent from the market. It should be noted that in reality, there is a wider number of factors to consider when making this judgement. Perhaps you need specialized talent and the local universities are producing graduates in this rare field. This is where a role typically difficult to fill has less risk than it may have for competitors not located in the same area. As an example to the contrary, perhaps your company is in an area of the country which is less desirable as a work location because of crime, weather or the local culture. In this case, the desired skill sets may be less rare in the overall market, but the difficulty comes in attracting people to the area.

As you work through the various roles within your company and populate the matrix, the four quadrants in the grid then serve as a prioritization of your "roles of interest." Those roles in the upper-right quadrant should be where your immediate strategic workforce planning efforts are concentrated.

The advantage of this method is that it is simple and would be easy to explain to those involved in the role analysis discussions. The disadvantage is that it is not forward-looking.

This is only one method of role segmentation to be considered. Several others are presented in the following pages.

A second approach followed by another company was to segment the business processes and to use the results to drive the role segmentation. For each role segment, a corresponding action is defined. In this way, this procedure not only segments the roles (Step 1 in our overall strategic workforce planning process, "Determine the roles of interest") but also sets the high level action plan (Step 5 in our strategic workforce planning process, "Establish action plans").

Roles that drive the strategy are strengthened while roles that are misaligned with the strategy call for redeployment of resources. A summary of all four segments and their related actions is shown below.

Role Type	Role Category	Resulting Action
Roles that drive the strategy	Strategic	Strengthen
Roles that support the strategic core	Core	Protect
Roles that need to be in place to support the strategy	Necessary	Streamline / outsource
Roles that are misaligned with the strategy	Misaligned	Redeploy

There may be some confusion between the two groups called "core" and "necessary." Core positions are the ones that directly support the strategic core whereas the necessary roles are not strategic but need to be in place for the strategy to move forward. The necessary positions don't need to be in-house resources. There may be an opportunity to outsource these resources or streamline the services they provide.

The advantages of this method are its strong link to strategy and the simplicity of yielding only four categories. The disadvantage is that it is not explicitly forward-looking although the strong link to the strategy could provide the forward view if the strategic plan of several years is used in this assessment and not just a one year outlook.

Another approach, presented in "The Differentiated Workforce" (Becker, 2009), provides a method by which the roles of the organization are segmented into A, B and C groups. The A positions are the strategic roles.

Becker's process begins with an organization's answer to two questions:

1. How will we compete?
2. What must we do exceptionally well to win?

He refers to these as an organization's strategic choice and an organization's strategic capabilities. These questions form the first two steps of his process.

The third step is to identify the strategic positions by selecting those roles which have a significant impact on one or more of the strategic capabilities. Recall that these capabilities were identified by answering the question, "What must we do exceptionally well to win?"

Further, once the roles affecting strategic capabilities have been identified, strategic positions are those that are characterized by a significant amount of variability in the performance levels of employees in these jobs. Some companies identify strategic roles as all positions affecting the successful execution of the business strategy, but Becker's process takes it one step further by selecting only the subset of those positions with large performance variability. The logic behind this is that any positions that do not have large performance variability have minimal opportunity for improvement and hence minimal impact on improving a company's performance. In this way, his method guides you toward concentrating your efforts on the roles where improvements will yield the largest benefit.

Another important aspect of Becker's method is that his process clearly outlines that you should "assess each role for present and future wealth-creation impact." In this way, he emphasizes that the process of strategic workforce planning is about planning for the future. Those leading the strategic workforce planning efforts for their organization will find that it is a difficult enough task to guide a company's leadership team to assess the positions of today. It is even more difficult to guide the leadership to envision what these roles need to be in the future.

To summarize Becker's process so far, we have the following steps:

1. Assess the strategic choice (How will we compete?)
2. Identify strategic capabilities (What must we do exceptionally well to win?)
3. Identify strategic positions (for present and future wealth impact).

Becker's process has two remaining steps, which do not fall under our framework Step 1 of "Determining Roles of Interest." They align with Steps 4 and 5 of our framework, namely, "Perform Gap Assessments" and "Establish Action Plans." Becker's final steps identify the behaviours which classify these employees as A, B, or C players within these "A" roles and goes on to recommend removing C players from A positions, placing A players in the A positions and setting development targets for B players in A positions.

Overall, Becker's process is quite impressive in that it displays a strong link to competitive advantage and considers how much improvement can be gained for the required effort.

One very significant caution is outlined by Becker, which is that,

> managers might place too much emphasis on senior positions and not enough on the entry-level, customer-facing positions. We suggest that managers follow our process to ensure that they identify the truly strategic roles in their business, not just the obvious ones.

I have experienced this very scenario in a large company where the only attempt to date to determine strategic roles was to assess each of the leadership positions. The company was attempting to focus its efforts on what they felt were the more significant positions, but in doing so essentially neglected all strategic positions below the leadership level.

When it comes to assessing strategic roles or "roles of interest," we have yet to consider who performs this assessment. In Becker's process, he recommends that an executive team determine the strategic choice and the strategic capabilities and that this executive team in cooperation with line managers and HR, identify the strategic positions. In most companies, it would be HR who would facilitate the entire process. In some companies, it may be facilitated by a centralized strategy team.

Another approach to determining roles of interest was presented by the Human Capital Institute (HCI) (Institute, 2010). Some key questions presented by HCI for this activity are:

- Which roles contribute more to strategic execution?
- Which roles have the potential to accelerate achievement of the business strategy?
- Which competencies are vital to executing strategy?

This approach offers a categorization of roles into four groups and HCI provides a guideline of the rough percentage of all of a company's roles which could fall into each category.

Category	Description	Percentage
Critical	Those roles vital for achieving strategic goals. Future success is compromised if these roles are not filled with extremely capable people.	10-15%
Core	Those roles relating to operational excellence. Current success is compromised if there are issues in critical roles.	20-25%
Supportive	Those roles that keep the internal operation working smoothly.	60-70%
Misaligned	Employees in these roles can be redeployed and the roles may be outsourced.	

There are quite a few companies and large consulting firms who have adopted this grouping of four categories, although you will find that they label them differently.

For the percentages of roles in each category, it is my opinion that this will vary far more than the ranges presented by HCI, especially when comparing high-tech and quickly changing industries to mature organizations whose products or services are becoming commodities.

These ranges do provide a rough guideline to the strategic workforce planning leader who is experiencing a leadership team which tends to think that far too many positions are critical. In this case, the leader driving the workforce planning function will have to take special care when creating the definition of a critical role for the organization. It may be best in this case to provide a checklist tool which defines a critical role rather than having the leadership make that determination.

In addition to the above methods, another view of role segmentation views the roles in an organization through a lens of complexity and criticality (Crucible Roles Business Case, 2011). Determining the complexity of the role is guided by whether the role impacts the top or bottom line results, whether the role is linked to growth opportunities, a turnaround initiative, valuable customers or critical internal audiences.

The criticality of the role is also assessed by a series of questions governing whether the role is required to work across organizational boundaries, has broad decision-making authority, develops strategy, requires a broad range of skills and requires the ability to adapt to changing circumstances.

Using this method, roles which are high in both complexity and criticality are the critical roles. Comparing this method to the "Difficulty to Obtain / Importance to the Business" matrix method previously presented, we can see the similarity in thought processes. Roles that are complex are likely difficult to obtain in the market and roles with high criticality are important to the business. Essentially these two methods will yield a similar result so selecting one of these to use in your own organization comes down to which set of language your leaders will be more comfortable using.

Boudreau and Ramstad (Ramstad, 2007) presented an HR decision framework in the book, *Beyond HR* which examines an organization through a variety of lenses. Contained within that framework is a method for determining pivotal roles.

Similar to Becker's process, Boudreau and Ramstad's framework begins with a true understanding of the business strategy. The framework then seeks to find "where specific improvements in the performance of the organization and talent most enhance sustainable strategic success." Some guiding questions for determining pivotal roles are:

- What resources do you have that your competitors would most like to have?
- Where would more and / or better people have the greatest effect?

Examining these questions, we can see additional similarities between this framework and that presented by Becker. Boudreau and Ramstad's framework encompasses far more as it goes on to examine the impact of processes, policies and culture.

On the talent side, once the pivotal positions are identified, this framework goes down one more level to examine which competencies within those roles are what make them pivotal. These are the competencies that an organization needs to develop and protect.

One final method from the CLC (Guide to Prioritizing Critical Employee Segments for Workplace Planning, 2010) provides guiding questions related to the criticality and difficulty of sourcing and /or training employees. The criticality focuses on revenue, innovation and business processes. The difficulty level focuses on scarcity of skills and costs associated with obtaining or developing these skills.

Criticality Considerations	Difficulty in Sourcing / Training
Level of impact on bottom-line results	Difficulty in sourcing skills
Level of involvement in developing growth opportunities	Magnitude of costs involved in hiring
Level of involvement in developing new products	Magnitude of costs involved in training
Level of involvement in optimizing business processes	Level of future availability of the skills required

Level of involvement in process outcomes which improve revenue	Degree of specialized skills or knowledge required
Risk to business performance if the role is left vacant	Current market value (compensation)
Level of influence on other critical business positions	Level of competition for this role in the market

This method assigns a score on a scale of 1 (very low) to 5 (very high) for each of the guiding questions. Scores are summed to create a total criticality score which ranges from 15-75. This range is split into three sub-ranges which places the role into one of three priority levels with associated recommended actions.

Priority	Action
1: Most critical due to their impact on business performance, degree of specialization, market value and associated costs.	Prioritize workforce planning resources to ensure that all positions are occupied. Consider all talent management options including hiring, training or realigning staff to address talent gaps.
2: Secondary priority. These roles maintain a medium to high criticality.	Assess options of hiring, redeploying and up-skilling to fill gaps and select low-cost options.
3: Least critical for business performance and typically low skill level.	Consider outsourcing and other low-cost options for addressing talent gaps.

A benefit of this method is that it has a forward-looking component (level of future availability of the skills). However, it has no assessment of whether you actually <u>need</u> those skills in the future. Further, an average score of 3.7 on each factor (moderate to high rating) will place the role in the highest priority. This may yield too many critical roles to manage, especially since most of the criticality questions appear to be highly subjective. This concern would be magnified in larger organizations.

Now that we've seen several ways for determining the roles of interest, the question remains, "which method is right for my company?" This is where you need to know your company very well and to know your people. How objective will your executive team be when it comes to answering some of the questions identified in these methods? What is the size of your company? The larger it is, the less likely a cross-functional executive team (facilitated by HR) will have insight into all of the roles you are trying to assess for strategic impact. The side effect of this is that those farther away from that area will tend to yield to the expertise of those who run that functional area. The leaders who run that functional area are likely to view their organization as very important since they don't have a good view of what the other functional areas contribute in terms of strategic execution.

Additionally, I will reiterate the caution of using the phrase critical role or pivotal role. Knowing the leadership of several companies, I tend to refer to this role segmentation step as "determining the roles of interest in order to determine actions <u>for workforce planning,</u>" i.e. not for any other purpose. When I focus on the fact that these activities are for the purpose of directing our efforts toward the most needed workforce and workforce plans (recruiting, talent development), I anticipate more objective discussions like "we really need to make sure we have a constant pipeline of specialized engineers." Referencing roles as critical is more likely to yield a view that "all leadership roles are critical since we execute the strategy." There is something in human nature where people need to feel "critical" or more importantly, not feel "non-critical" especially during uncertain economic times where the fear of downsizing is present.

I will conclude with my own tool for establishing "roles of interest" where the first step begins with a conversation. This conversation is between HR and the internal customer. The tool is a combination of what I feel are the most significant considerations from the methods presented previously in this chapter.

The HR representative in the conversation should be familiar with strategic workforce planning and should act as the facilitator.

The exact position of the internal customer can vary. In smaller companies, it may be a general manager; in larger companies, it may be the head of a business unit, Vice President or Sr. Vice President. In any case, the person representing the internal customer needs to be familiar with the roles within that part of the organization and any past challenges related to specific positions.

The purpose of the conversation is for the HR facilitator to understand the priorities of this area of the business as it relates to executing the strategy. A few key questions are:

- What are the key business objectives for the next five years?
- What strengths do we have that we need to protect from our competitors?
- What new strengths do we need to establish in order to maintain our competitive edge?

Once HR understands the strategic direction and the strengths which arise from the above questions, these answers need to be translated into critical talent needs.

A few questions come to mind:

- Which roles are involved in executing the business objectives?
- Which roles are associated with the strengths we need to protect?
- Which new roles need to be in place to establish the new strengths identified?

Finally, depending on the workforce planning resources you have available, you may have to prioritize the critical roles with the following questions:

- Of the roles identified, which (if any) develop strategy?
- Of the roles identified, where will a shortage of employees impact strategic execution the most?
- Of the roles identified, where will a shortage of employees impact our competitive strengths the most?
- Of the roles identified, where will a shortage of employees impact our financial performance the most?

If you'd like an additional level of sophistication, once you have established your prioritized list of roles, consider the underlying competencies which are most important. You can try to assess that in this stage of the process or you can cover this as part of your action plan determination.

My own tool is shown on the following page (without the competency considerations) and is also listed in the appendices for easy access. In creating my own tool, I have selected the aspects of multiple methods that I felt were of the most value in obtaining objective assessments for the "roles of interest."

SWP Conversation Guideline for Determining "Roles of Interest"

What is a "role of interest?"

A role of interest is one which is connected to strategic execution and/or maintaining our competitive strengths, now and in the near future. These positions are flagged by Strategic Workforce Planning as those requiring prioritized attention in order to maintain a supply of "the right" talent.

Step 1: Role Identification

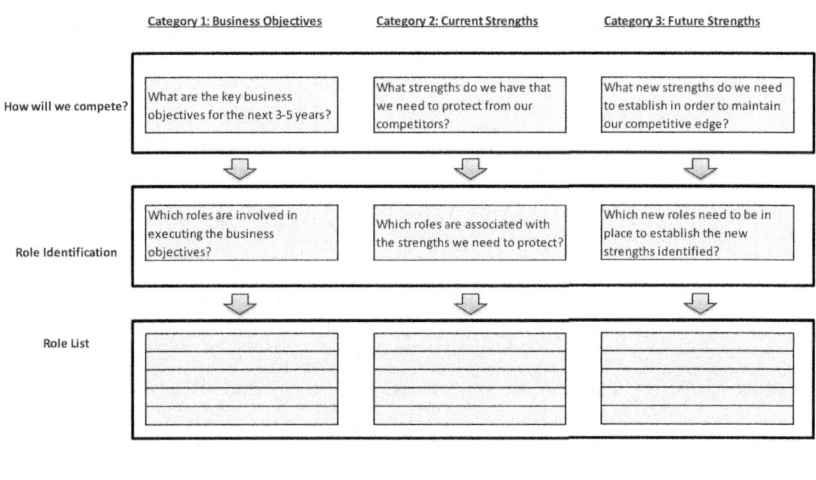

Step 2: Role Prioritization

Note: This step is performed on the list of roles identified above. This step can be optional if the list of roles above is fairly short.

1. Of the roles identified, which (if any) develop strategy?

2. Of the roles identified, where will a shortage of employees impact strategic execution the most?

3. Of the roles identified, where will a shortage of employees impact our competitive strengths the most?

4. Of the roles identified, where will a shortage of employees impact our financial performance the most?

Figure 6: Tool for Assessing Roles of Interest

Step 2: Establish the Current State

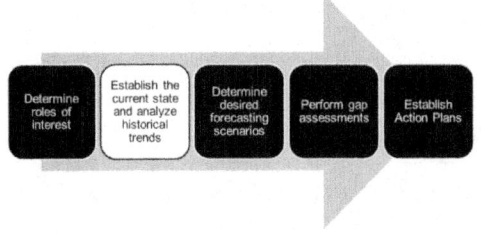

Establishing the <u>current state is not just about today</u>. It's also very important to know how you got there. What significant business events occurred in the past? Which of these events will impact the future? This type of information will become even more significant in the next step of the framework when projecting modeling data forward.

It is not necessary to look too far into the past. I have seen some workforce planning tools which propose capturing significant business events going back decades. From my own experience, this is not necessary. The timeline of workforce planning is in line with the timeline of the business plan which, for most organizations, is three to five years. Most workforce planning activities focus on the immediate time frame up to about five years. For those modeling the workforce in North America, you have probably noticed from examining your own data that the human capital statistics you see today are quite different than the few years leading up to 2008. As you gain experience in workforce planning, you will quickly learn which events in your company are the ones that matter most and which areas of the company were impacted. Also keep in mind that significant events in the past may have affected some of your critical roles and not others.

Let's take a look at a fictional company as an example. This company has completed Step 1 of the strategic workforce planning framework and has determined it's "roles of interest."

For simplicity, let's select the following two roles:

- electrical engineers, and
- technical sales representatives.

Suppose that in 2007, this company purchased an engineering consulting house and merged its existing electrical engineers with the engineers from the purchased company. This change affected the engineering role but did not impact the technical sales role.

Suppose that in 2008, like many companies, this company saw a substantial decrease in its revenue. The company decided to downsize some of its sales representatives since the number of customers had decreased. On the other hand, since the engineers were responsible for designing the products of the future and maintaining the technical aspects of existing products, the company decided not to impact the engineering roles. This would be an example of a past event impacting only the sales positions.

Suppose also in 2008, the impact from an economic decline (not surprisingly) had forced many people to hold off on their retirement plans and work a few extra years. This would be an example of a past event which would impact both roles.

It might be a good idea to create a master list of all significant past events and then determine the impact those events had on the role you are examining. However, for large global companies you will have events impacting certain global regions and not others, so an extra column recording the impacted region is recommended. A sample tool for recording these events with a few examples is shown in Figure 7: Master List of Past Events and Associated Role Impact.

Master List of Significant Events

This tool is designed to guide you through recording significant events in the company history which impact the projection methods of past trends.

Step 1: Enter a brief description of the past event.

Step 2: Record the date on which the event took place.

Step 3: Record the impacted roles.

Step 4: Record the impacted regions.

Past Event	Date	Impacted Roles	Impacted Region
Economic downturn	Nov. 2008	All hourly roles	USA
Outsourcing	Feb. 2010	Accounts payable roles	Canada, USA
Restructuring (Voluntary Packages)	Apr. 2011	IT, Sales	Germany

Figure 7: Master List of Past Events and Associated Role Impact

As a final thought, I offer the following visual to assist in picturing the significant events of your company. This visual (Figure 8: Sample headcount chart with significant business events) is a simple depiction of the historical headcount values associated with our two sample "roles of interest" with significant events from the past noted in the timeline. When it comes to projecting numbers forward in an intelligent way, this information will be valuable.

In this simple example, we have shown only events which add or subtract headcount to the role in question. The range of possible events is far more varied than this example. Suppose a company redefines a role to make it more strategic and it adds new skill set requirements to that role. This neither adds nor subtracts headcount in the immediate term but it is an event recommended for capture on the timeline in case a piece of data such as turnover starts to rise. Visualizing the event on the timeline allows you to have it handy if, after collecting your historical data, you find a trend after this date which requires explanation.

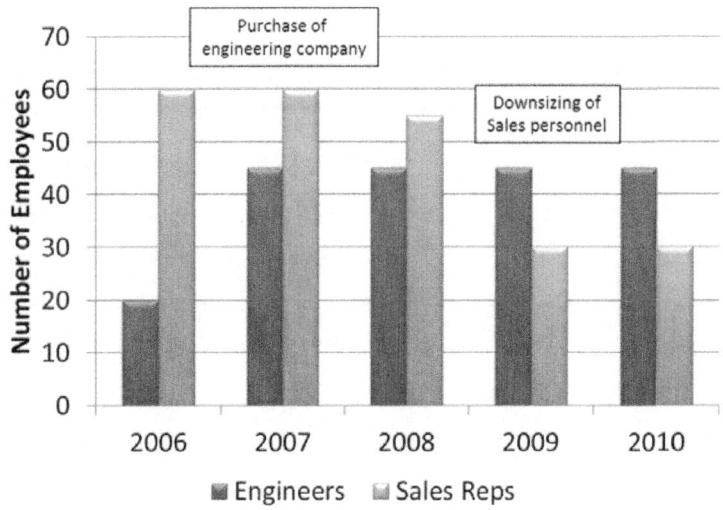

Figure 8: Sample headcount chart with significant business events

Step 3: Determine Desired Forecasting Scenarios

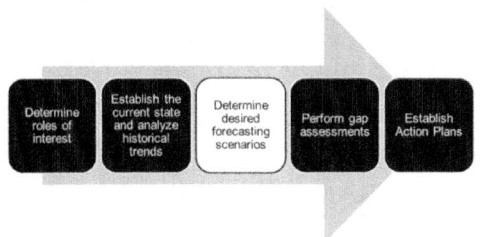

This step involves determining and running desired scenarios of the future. Since there are always business uncertainties (markets, industries, environments, technology changes, etc.), scenario planning is essentially a tool used for making better business decisions in relation to possible uncertainties. Suppose

41

you anticipate growing your business by 10% in the next year. If you planned for this one scenario, you would have no room for error. What happens if your business only grows by 2%? Perhaps it may grow by 15%? How will that impact your business? How will that impact your human capital plan? Do you have enough flexibility in your workforce to handle all of these cases?

For these reasons, scenario planning is not a pure science. It comes down to a combination of data analysis, research regarding areas of uncertainty and experience. The intent here is not to try to model your entire company. Recall that we determined the "roles of interest" in Step 1 of our workforce planning framework, so the focus is on these roles. Of course the uncertainty impacting these roles can be broad-reaching like industry-shaping forces which will impact multiple roles, or it could be a change in technology which may render a previously strategic role obsolete.

The list of scenarios looks at several possible futures. Scenarios can be used to forecast future demand of talent and can also forecast future supply. Shell describes their scenario planning as follows:

> Shell uses scenarios to explore the future. Our scenarios are not mechanical forecasts. They recognise that people hold beliefs and make choices that can lead down different paths. They reveal different possible futures that are plausible and challenge people's assumptions (Shell Scenarios: See What the Future Might Look Like, 2012).

> Who determines the scenarios? Like the discussion about determining roles of interest, there should be a discussion between HR and their internal customers in order to form a joint

list of scenarios. If HR tries to develop these scenarios on their own, they are less likely to be viewed as credible.

There may also be organizational considerations when it comes to scenario planning. If the business is large enough to have its own centralized strategic planning group, the factors affecting the business have already been analyzed in order to produce the strategic objectives and the financial plans. In this case, HR would be holding the discussion with this planning group in addition to the internal customer. In fact, in some companies, the entire workforce planning function is part of this strategic planning group whereas in about 80% of companies, strategic workforce planning resides in HR and may be combined with the HR analytics function.

So how do we decide which possible futures interest us with this discussion? With the business strategy always in mind, here are a few recommendations.

1. Establish a list of the driving forces affecting your businesses. Some companies find a SWOT (strengths, weaknesses, opportunities and threats) analysis useful at this stage to identify the driving forces.
2. Determine which ones will impact your business the most.
3. What range of impact will they have on the variables in your scenario?
4. Create your list of possible scenarios based on the information above.

As you head into your first experience with scenarios planning, avoid some of the pitfalls for beginners. Some great guidance on this was provided in a 2009 article by Charles Roxburgh (Roxburgh, 2009). The most important points are listed below.

- Don't become paralyzed. In this the author cautions that faced with a wide range of scenarios, people don't know how to deal with the magnitude of the problem. He recommends picking the scenarios with the most likely outcomes.
- Don't let scenarios muddy communications, i.e., don't let the multiple futures interfere with the one vision being communicated by your leadership.
- Don't rely on an excessively narrow set of outcomes. By this, the author cautions that too narrow a set of scenarios may give you a false sense of security.
- Remember when to avoid scenarios altogether. When uncertainty is very high and scenario planning is highly unlikely to produce an accurate result, there is no value in moving forward. Looking back to the market decline in 2008, the uncertainty of the future was so large that several Fortune 100 companies announced on their earnings calls that they would not make a projection of the future.

There are four main categories of scenarios which can be developed: inductive, deductive, incremental and normative.

Inductive scenarios take a look at the major drivers of change and trends which are likely to affect a company. This method starts at an existing point and then uses the driving forces to project the possible futures.

Deductive scenario planning, in its simplest form, selects two major drivers of change and then creates four scenarios based on how those drivers converge. Envision a two by two matrix producing four scenario options. Potential drivers can be social (e.g. crime rates), technological (computer innovations), environmental, economical, etc.

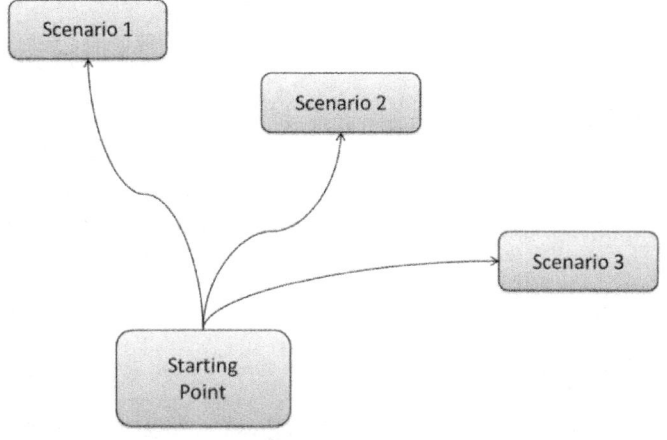

Figure 9: Inductive Scenario Planning

Retirement ages increase Health care regulations unchanged	Retirement ages increase Health care regulations repealed
Retirement ages decrease Health care regulations unchanged	Retirement ages decrease Health care regulations repealed

Social (left vertical axis)

Political

Figure 10: Deductive Scenario Planning

For more complex scenario mapping, some planners overlay multiple factors on each axis of the grid. The key in this case would be to group drivers that have a similar impact on your business.

For this method, brainstorming sessions for a list of potential drivers can be led by strategy experts. Where these experts reside in a company can vary substantially with the organization's structure or they may be absent altogether. In the latter case, an external expert is recommended to facilitate the discussions.

Once a list of potential drivers has been formed, the discussion turns to questions such as:

- Which forces are most likely to significantly change the direction of the business?
- Which changes in these forces seem inevitable?

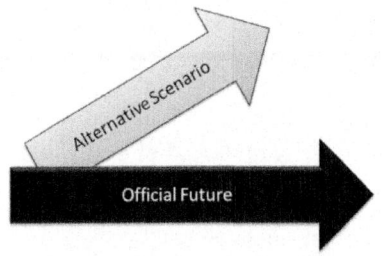

Figure 11: Incremental Scenario Planning

Incremental scenarios take a look at the "official future" and then consider ways in which the future might be altered. The "official future" is the one written into the business plans. In this way, the future in the business plan is viewed as the most probable future and the alterations are the risks associated with variations from the most probable future. The alterations considered are the ones which would send the business in a substantially different direction.

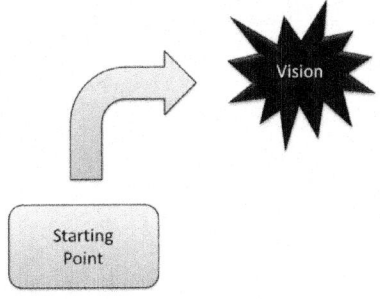

Figure 12: Normative Scenario Planning

Normative scenarios create a desirable outcome for the company. The challenge then becomes planning to achieve it. This method of scenario planning was more popular in the 1960s and 1970s than it is today since it is based more on a vision than a strategic assessment of what impacts the business. The goals are defined more in terms of what the business wants to see happen rather than what they think is most likely to happen.

As an additional reference, Paul J. H. Schoemaker (Eyes Wide Open: Embracing Uncertainty Through Scenario Panning, 2009), comments that "when managers are facing the profound uncertainties increasingly seen today, they tend to adopt one of three strategic postures."

The first option he outlines is the "zero-option." Essentially this is the "do nothing" option where leadership waits for uncertainty to dissipate. Given current levels of global uncertainty and the low probability of it going away any time soon, this isn't an option I would recommend to anyone.

The second approach is to "bet strongly on one particular future" which allows leadership to convey a clear goal to the employees. This approach seems most similar to the normative approach previously presented in that it has a primary vision but it is combined with an "official future" from the incremental approach.

The third approach is described as "a deliberate attempt to separate what we do and what we do not know about the future." From here, possible scenarios relative to the uncertainties are explored in order to map out possible futures. This approach is somewhat like the deductive method with multiple drivers because the following steps are recommended:

- Identify the central question,
- Identify the driving forces and systemic changes underway,
- Identify the forces which will have the greatest impact on your future, and
- Use this information in strategic business decision making.

Schoemaker and others have observed trends toward using this third approach.

I will conclude this section by presenting a tool of my own which follows the strategic workforce planning framework I presented in an earlier chapter (Figure 5: Author's Strategic Workforce Planning Framework). Recall that in the first two steps of the framework, the "roles of interest" were determined and an evaluation of the current state was completed. Now, using each of the "roles of interest," determine the list of potential changes which can impact those roles.

You can see from the tool shown (Figure 13: Sample Scenario Development Tool) that the categories are similar to those you would use to conduct scenario planning on your entire business. This is because, as Figure 5 suggests, the business strategy drives this step of the strategic workforce planning framework.

Scenario Development Tool

This tool is designed to guide you through developing a list of scenarios for each of your "roles of interest."

Step 1: From the list you developed in the "Determine Roles of Interest" step of the Strategic Workforce Planning framework, select one role to be the focus of this tool. The intent is to use this tool for each "role of interest."

Step 2: Conduct a meeting with internal customers related to this role and brainstorm the anticipated changes which may impact the future of this role.

Step 3: Record the resulting scenario plans needed to assess the impact of anticipated changes.

Role Segment:

Categories of Potential Changes Impacting this Role	Anticipated Changes Impacting This Role	Resulting Scenario Plans for Simulation
Business growth		
Competency changes		
Geographic considerations		
Technological changes		
Structural changes		
Business process changes		
Market changes		
Social changes		
Other		

Figure 13: Sample Scenario Development Tool

In this framework, scenario planning on the entire business was conducted previously in order to document the business strategy and objectives. Within this step of the framework, we concentrate on scenarios and their impact to the strategic roles, not the entire company.

Depending on your company structure, this activity is likely conducted as a discussion between HR and the business partner. For some companies, it may be led by a central strategic function if one exists. The discussion is centered on those potential changes considered significant enough to impact the "roles of interest."

The type of impact can be quite varied. Let's look at a sales position as an example and determine the possible scenarios related to potential changes. Under business growth, perhaps you anticipate a range of 10-20% growth in the coming year. This impacts the number of sales people you will need which would lead you into a headcount model at this stage of the workforce planning framework and a headcount gap assessment in the next step of the framework.

Suppose you also anticipate technological changes related to the products you offer. This could impact the technical competencies you require of your sales people in order for them to be qualified to sell the products. This would lead you into a competency model in this stage and a competency gap assessment in the next stage. Keep in mind that it is very possible that you may have both of these impacts and hence gap assessments of both headcount and competencies.

For geographic considerations, perhaps your business strategy is driving you to move your workforce from higher cost locations to cheaper ones. This is a popular issue with global companies. With this impact, you will head into possible mobility models and a gap assessment on the workforce that can and cannot be shifted. In the final state of the workforce planning framework, "Establish Action Plans," this situation becomes quite complex depending on the labour laws and other regulatory considerations. Anticipate a longer scenario planning activity and a longer implementation timeline.

Step 4: Perform Gap Assessments

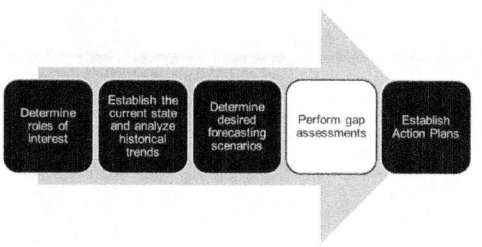

The step for performing gap assessments in the workforce planning process is sometimes confusing for those who came from headcount or manpower planning so the following statement will clarify the gaps we are considering.

In a previous phase of the workforce planning evolution, we would have considered only the gap in the headcount we have today and what we need in the immediate future. In strategic workforce planning, there are two types of gaps. The first gap is indeed the gap in headcount although the timespan is probably three to five years instead of the short term. The second gap is where the process gets a lot more intelligent since we assess the gap between the competencies we have today and the competencies we need in the future.

It is actually quite possible to have a headcount gap of zero but a large gap in the competencies required. A great example of this is when the skill sets within a specific role need to change over time. Consider a company who years ago had 50 computer programmers coding Fortran or Cobol. They may still need 50 programmers today and in the future, but it is unlikely that the skills they seek have much to do with Fortran and Cobol. To close the competency gap, this company would have had to have had the foresight to develop modern programming skills in these employees or hire new programmers from the outside.

Another example of this can be seen in some Human Resources departments. Traditionally, HR representatives supporting employees were very transactional in their relationship with employees. They interpreted company policy, perhaps processed tuition reimbursement forms and collected forms pertaining to company benefits.

In more recent times, a transition of these employees into employee coaches is becoming more evident. The competency gap in this case is that the skill sets required to be transactional are not the same skill sets required to provide effective coaching. Companies are faced with the same choice as the IT example above: develop the current employees or hire new ones from the outside. Most companies would prefer to develop their current employees whenever possible since these employees already have knowledge of the company and in this HR example, have already established relationships with the employees they support.

Let's take a look at a simple example to demonstrate one possible tool to use for performing gap assessments. Let's consider the role of the IT programmer. First, we'll examine the headcount gap. Then we'll consider the competency gap.

In Step 3 of the strategic workforce planning framework, we would have generated a variety of scenarios. For this particular example, (Figure 14: Sample Headcount Model) the company's five year plan includes an objective to replace several of its legacy systems with new systems. This is a common challenge facing many companies today.

The company would like to hire two leaders today to coordinate these efforts and 31 extra programmers in Year 1 to create the new systems. As the new systems are created, the old systems will be retired. This means the workload of the employees supporting the old systems will be eliminated.

Figure 14 shows a mathematical model. Based on natural attrition rates, retirement predictions and internal career moves, the number of people left in this role can be projected. This is our internal supply.

While this example only shows one year of historical data in order to display within the width of the page, I generally go back about five years in order to make an intelligent judgement of how to project the numbers forward. For companies in the U.S., you may find that the historical data prior to 2008 has different patterns than data post 2008.

Sample Workforce Forecasting Model Role: IT Programmers	Historical Data		Future Headcount				
	1 Year Ago	Today	Year 1	Year 2	Year 3	Year 4	Year 5
Total Headcount at start of Fiscal Year		147	149	180	160	145	145
Retirement Estimates							
Will Have Reached Retirement Age		30	35	42	44	49	55
Percentage Anticipated to Retire	4.8%	5.4%	5.1%	5.4%	5.6%	5.9%	6.1%
Total Estimated Retirements		8	8	10	9	9	9
Losses by Non-retirement Methods							
Estimated Reduction by Turnover		7	7	8	7	6	6
Estimated Reduction by Internal Moves		5	5	6	5	5	5
Total Non-retirement Losses		12	12	14	12	11	11
Total Losses During the Year		20	20	24	21	20	20
Headcount Needs for Significant Events							
New hires to program new systems		2	31				
Release of employees supporting old systems				(20)	(15)		
Total Recruitment Needs		22	51	4	6	20	20

Figure 14: Sample Headcount Model

To provide some assistance in reading Figure 14, start by looking at the column called "Today." Today, the company has 147 IT programmers. Based on historical retirement rates and the growing pool of people in the retirement category, the company anticipates eight people retiring during the year.

Continuing down the same column, the company predicts that seven additional people will leave the company for reasons other than retirement. Additionally, five people are anticipated to leave the IT programmer role for other opportunities inside the company. In total, the company surmises that it will lose a total of twenty IT programmers this year.

For the headcount impact of significant events recorded in this model, the company anticipates hiring two IT leaders to oversee the programming of the new systems. Therefore, the recruitment team anticipates a hiring volume of 22 people in order to meet the company's objectives related to this role.

In the next year, the company starts with a headcount of 149 programmers. Essentially, they replaced all vacancies and added two new positions. They anticipate losing a total of 20 programmers by "normal means" but also predict that they will need 31 new programmers to start building the new systems. The total recruitment volume is therefore 51 people in order to meet the total headcount requirement of 180 programmers for the next year. This total headcount is our demand. Our headcount gap by the end of Year 1 is 51 people.

Year 2 gets a bit more interesting and this is where the scenario gets specific in its actions. The company starts with a total headcount of 180 programmers. It anticipates losing 24 employees through natural attrition and internal moves. It also anticipates that the workload of 20 programmers will be eliminated with the completion of some of the new systems. Since the total recruitment needs for that year is shown to be only four people, this scenario is clearly one which absorbs the employees whose workload was eliminated and retains them to work on other projects. As workload is eliminated, these workers are used to replace those who have left by attrition, retirement and internal career moves.

Year 3 is similar in its actions as the company completes more of the new systems and the workload of 15 more programmers is eliminated. Again, this scenario absorbs these employees and retains them in the IT programmer role.

An additional scenario which may have been run in Step 3 of the strategic workforce planning framework is the one in which programmers whose work is eliminated are simply let go. In this case, the total recruitment needs on the bottom line would be larger in Years 2 and 3. It would not be unusual for a company to look at both of these scenarios for IT-related jobs. The first scenario buys needed talent in Year 1 but develops talent internally in Years 2 and 3. In the latter scenario, all of the talent is bought as redundant internal talent is let go.

This model is small and simple for demonstration purposes. In real applications, they can get complex. The section on significant events could contain a wide variety of events such as:

- acquisitions,
- consolidations, and
- opening new locations.

Additional impacts to headcount which can be added to the model are:

- revenue growth / decline forecasts (to keep headcount in line with revenue), and
- efficiency gains.

The mathematical model presented above focuses on the headcount gap but does give some hint of the need to assess the competency gap. As mentioned, this scenario absorbs the redundant talent and uses them on new projects. Given that this talent previously programmed old legacy systems, it is highly unlikely that they are skilled in programming the new systems. Programming languages have changed over time and unless these employees have taught themselves these new languages, they are now lacking the skills needed for the future.

On the other hand, these employees know how the company works, are assimilated into its culture, have established relations throughout the company and the logic behind programming different languages can be quite similar. This is where a competency gap assessment becomes very useful.

Gap assessments examine the competencies and skill sets of today and compare them to the competencies and skill sets needed tomorrow. In this case, a portion of the gap assessment for the IT programmer role could look like Figure 15: Competency Gap Worksheet.

I will discuss ways to close the workforce planning gap in the next section since this falls under the next step of establishing action plans.

Strategic Objective	Skills Today	Skills Needed Tomorrow
Creation and Support of New IT Systems	Project Management	Project Management
	Internal Relationships	Internal Relationships
	Cobol, Fortran	C++, C#
	Time Management	Time management
		Process improvement

Figure 15: Competency Gap Worksheet

Step 5: Establish Action Plans

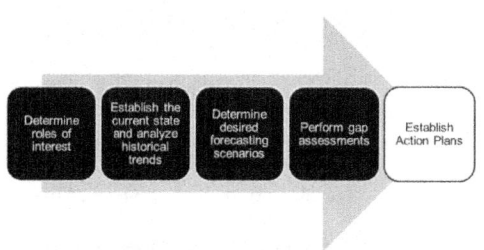

Before we discuss possible action plans, let's review the entire strategic workforce planning framework to recall what we have done so far. The detailed image provided will assist you (Figure 16: Details of Strategic Workforce Planning Framework).

First, we recognized that the business strategy drives the entire process. This strategy determines the business objectives. With this in mind, we established a tool with which we could determine the "roles of interest." These roles are linked to the strategy and are a source of competitive advantage both today and in the future. Establishing a prioritized list of these roles allows a company to focus its strategic workforce planning resources on the roles which will impact the future success of the business the most.

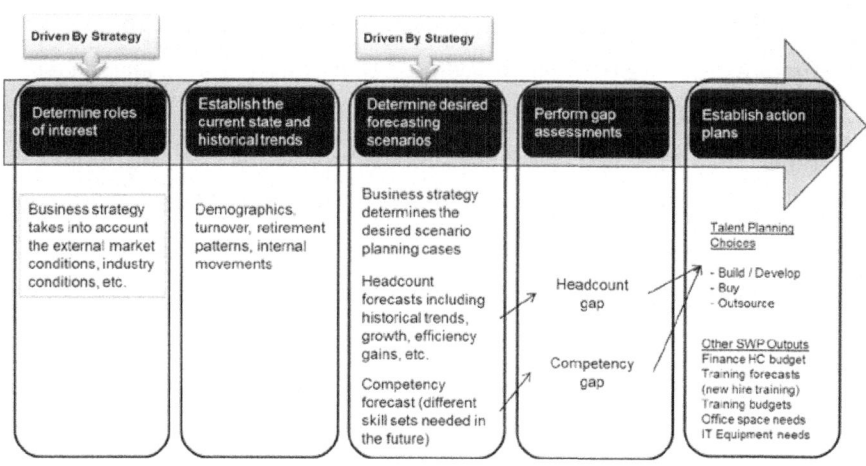

Figure 16: Details of Strategic Workforce Planning Framework

Next, we established the current state recognizing that it is not just about today but also about understanding the significant business events of the past. These past events provide information on why certain trends behaved in certain ways.

In Step 3 of the framework, the business strategy drives which future scenarios or "possible futures" should be those to which we dedicate an analysis. Using knowledge of the business strategy, environmental scanning and past trends, models of these future scenarios were built.

In Step 4, gap assessments were conducted. These assessments analyzed both the headcount and competency gaps. Now, in the final stage, decisions are made to address these gaps through action plans.

Looking back at the IT programmer example, there are several action plans. In the earlier years of the scenario model, your action plan is to buy the talent from the open market which means that your recruitment team needs to be involved and needs to understand your 5-year planning model. Additionally, since this means you will be hiring new employees, your training group should be informed so they know how many people require new hire training and when. Taking this a bit further, since the added positions in the earlier years are additional headcount instead of replacement headcount, your IT department would benefit from understanding the 5-year plan so they can project IT budgets for new computers, software packages and predict resources needed for installations. Your Finance department has an interest in your plan since the additional headcount impacts budgeting. Taking this even further, your benefits and finance groups are interested in this additional headcount in order to judge the financial and administrative impact of providing employee benefits. It becomes very clear just how many groups can benefit from this simple decision of "we're going to hire from the outside."

In the later years of our IT programmer example, we have the option of hiring from the outside or developing the programmers whose work was eliminated after the old systems were retired. Suppose you wish to develop the talent from your existing employee base. This requires putting development plans in place to ensure that those employees have the right skills by the time you need them.

For one final thought, if the company chose to let the redundant programmers go, your action plan would involve the people who coordinate outplacement services, possible buy-out offers etc.

Within some scenarios examined, there may be only one action plan needed. However, in the case of our IT programmers, we have multiple options, so there are some important aspects to consider.

A significant consideration in the action plan stage is the need to establish the cost associated with each action plan. Will it cost the company $3 million dollars to retrain its staff but cost much less to hire from the outside? What will be the impact on the loyalty of the remaining employees if you let their coworkers go instead of retraining them? There is certainly more to consider than the one-time cost of action plan implementation.

The next consideration is the risk associated with implementing the action plan. If it is determined that it is cheaper to buy the talent from the marketplace, is the talent actually available? This is part of the environmental scanning activity which will be described in the next section. I will demonstrate here why I do not explicitly identify environmental scanning as a separate step in strategic workforce planning.

The environmental scanning done in this example is of the external workforce. Depending on internal company processes and preferences, some companies may opt to assess the availability of this talent in the market as part of the scenario analysis. Others may choose to evaluate the scenario plans first and shorten the list of possible action plans before dedicating resources for this external scan. The same holds true for when a company would opt to put resources on the activity of assessing the cost of the action plan. Recall also that some environmental scanning (more on the business environment than the talent environment) would have been performed in the development of the business strategy.

For these reasons, I view "environmental scanning" as an activity which floats across the strategic workforce planning process and is visited several times throughout the entire process.

Environmental Scanning

When we took a look at scenario planning, we had two categories: scenario planning for drivers impacting the business and scenario planning for talent. Environmental scanning is conducted for both of these scenario planning types although the strategic workforce planning personnel may not be the group performing the environmental scan for the business if a company has a centralized strategy group. In this case, the workforce planning group would need to be in communication with the strategy team but would only be performing the additional scanning activities needed from the point of view of talent.

Keep in mind that environmental scanning is performed for both the internal and external environment and is not performed as a one-time activity. With experience, you will come to know which scanning activities should be performed frequently and which ones can cycle on a longer time frame before they need to be repeated. This repeated scanning will ensure that business planning and talent planning remain current. I think most people would agree that environmental scanning requirements have been required on a more frequent basis in recent years.

So, what benefits would be derived from environmental scanning? These types of activities help build a deeper understanding of how the business operates and what impacts its future success. Combining environmental scanning with the process of strategic workforce planning enables a company to build flexibility into its workforce in response to anticipated changes and variability.

Let's take a look at some of the environmental scanning considerations.

The political environment is one that impacts all companies regardless of whether you operate in one country or many. Changing government policies, tax laws, employee benefit requirements, etc. all have an impact on the business. Across country lines, the impact of these factors can be substantially different as well as the level of government stability.

Economic growth and decline, inflation, exchange rates and the phase of industry maturity impact both the business strategy and the talent strategy, so this scan is required in both cases. Again, if you have a central strategy team, these factors will have been considered in the formation of the business strategy but workforce planning leads need to be present in the strategy meetings in order to assess the potential impact to talent.

Changes in technology affect businesses in different ways. For users of technology, changes may provide efficiencies. These changes may make certain jobs redundant or substantially change the skill sets required. For creators of new technology, this represents rapidly changing product lines which impact the jobs associated with designing, producing, selling and distributing these products. Additionally, new product launches are one of the most difficult to forecast in terms of sales so these companies may have a wider range of variation in their business plan which needs to be considered for scenario planning.

The aging of employee demographics is one of the most popular topics today as companies plan for an increasing number of retirements in many countries. If your industry and company are fairly stable and mature, planning for this can be a manageable task. However, if your company is faced with this challenge in addition to rapid growth and changing technologies, strategic workforce planning becomes crucial to your success.

While we have discussed the impact of changing demographics on the employee base, keep in mind that those responsible for building the business strategy will also have to consider the changing demographics of their customer base which will impact consumer preferences.

To provide a brief summary of this topic, Figure 17: Environmental Scanning Activities) outlines possible environmental scanning activities. It provides some of the major categories but should not be considered an all-inclusive list.

This tool is designed as a reference for the various types of internal and external environmental scanning activities.

Internal	External
Employee demographics	Political stability
Employee tenure	Industry growth / maturity
Career development opportunities	Inflation
Trends for retirements and non-retirement turnover	Exchange rates
Employee engagement	Tax laws
Financial constraints	Consumer demographics
	Technology changes

Figure 17: Environmental Scanning Activities

3. Implementation

From extensive benchmarking, it is clear that truly incorporating strategic workforce planning into an organization is a journey of several years. It requires communication plans, resolution of data issues, the possible creation of new data sources, establishing the best technologies to support the program, researching external data sources, establishing internal relationships, aligning with existing HR strategy projects, etc. The list goes on. However, a company can begin to see the value that data insights can provide from launching the first few tools to its internal customers. This tends to drive interest in the topic more than a presentation of the business case.

As a dramatic example of this, many companies fear the oncoming wave of baby boomer retirements. For one company, their fear was the potential loss of much of its leadership who had been with the company many years. I helped them address this fear with a leadership dashboard which assigned a retirement risk to their leadership positions. Next, we linked in the available talent which had been assessed as "ready" for these leadership positions. Finally, we defined the overall risk of any leadership position to be a combination of these two.

What does this tell us? When we assessed the leadership under this risk definition, the risk to the overall continuity of the leadership was very small and the fears were diminished.

I defined a second level of high risk in this dashboard which also brought the company additional insight. This second category of risk is where you have talent "ready" but there is a very low chance of vacancy in the position for which they are ready. In these cases, you risk losing your top talent because they have nowhere to go. This is where HR and the employee's management can develop a talent plan for possible lateral moves to hold the employee's interest in the company.

There are two lessons in the example above. The first, as I mentioned above is that you can begin to derive value from a small number of strategic workforce planning tools. The second lesson is not to assume that the "reality of the masses" is the reality of your company. Always check these generalizations with your own data.

Selling the Concept

From the example at the beginning of the chapter, the importance of knowing the unique workforce challenges of your business is evident. There is an inherent danger in assuming that the issues presented by others are the same issues affecting your own business. That's not to say that you should ignore information from other sources, but certainly validate that it is applicable to your company.

Strategic workforce planning in many companies begins with the presentation of a business case to the leadership in order to gain support for the initiative. For smaller companies, this may consist of convincing a only a handful of leaders and can be done in one well-prepared meeting. For larger, global companies, this approach can be unmanageable and the approach needs to be more regionally focused.

Business cases from various companies have been presented in research forums and some workforce planning leaders aim to replicate these presentations for their own companies. The advice I provide here is that your business case needs to be very specific to your company's challenges and not just a general presentation of public survey results as your justification.

Let's take a look at a few approaches to building business cases. In Canada, the workforce demographics for postal delivery workers indicated that half of its workforce would retire within the next decade. Aging demographics is probably the number one justification for workforce planning today. For this company, the business case would be driven by the need to replace these workers. At the same time, these pending workforce changes would provide the company with the opportunity to reshape the workforce in line with its future business strategy. In short, Canada Post is not aiming to merely replace its retiring workforce; it is aiming to improve its strategic positioning at the same time.

For another approach, let's consider IT consulting companies who provide custom solutions to their customers. To serve their customers, these companies need to determine a customer's issues and then form a team which likely consists of hardware, software, service and project management experts. With a wide range of both historical and modern systems to support, these companies need to have a great amount of flexibility in their workforce. The driving justification for strategic workforce planning in these organizations is the need to access a wide range of technical knowledge and geographical availability. Essentially, the business case for these companies is based more on the skill sets, competencies and mobility of their workforce rather than concerns over age demographics. That's not to say that they may not also have an age demographic challenge as an additional justification.

As a third business case approach, let's consider a large company where a portion of that company exists in a mature market. Parts of the company may be in growth mode whereas other parts may be declining due to changes in technology. In this company, the justification for strategic workforce planning in the growth areas would likely be driven by the challenge of obtaining enough qualified employees to fill new positions. In the mature area of the company, the justification for workforce planning would be driven by the need to gain efficiencies in the business in order to maintain profitability.

These three approaches are not unique to any one company and one can easily locate dozens of approaches. The one thing common to all of these approaches is their link to the business strategy. Recall that the workforce planning framework presented near the beginning of this book illustrated that the linkage to the business strategy is a fundamental requirement before strategic workforce planning can be effective. With that in mind, a business case can be formulated to present the challenges that are specific to your organization.

One final challenge in creating your business case may reside within the workforce planning leader. Since 80% of companies embarking on the workforce planning journey have selected a member of Human Resources to lead the effort, this leader may not have the business acumen or a sufficient understanding of the business strategy to build an effective case. As an example, in some companies the lead is an organizational development professional. Depending on the reputation of this type of professional, the credibility of the workforce planning initiative can be affected. In some companies, these professionals are highly regarded, whereas in others, they are viewed as too theoretical to credibly address the real business world.

The three previous examples provided some of the more popular justifications for a business case, but you probably want to provide a lot more information before you will be able to convince your leadership that an investment is worthwhile. The following are a few suggestions.

If you can get access to historical revenue numbers, take a look at revenue over at least the past 5 years. If you are a public company, this is easy to obtain from the SEC filings. If you are a private company or you need to split up the revenue into divisions, you will need to have a good relationship with your financial team.

Next, get financial information on labour and associated costs. For public companies, you might use the SG&A numbers (Selling, General and Administrative Expenses) on the financial statements. Otherwise you need your finance team again.

Now overlay these values on a graph. Is the labour cost rising faster than revenue growth? Is the labour cost rising but your revenue has plateaued? If those two lines are approaching each other over time, labour expense is becoming a larger and larger percentage relative to the company's revenue and the driving motivation for workforce planning would be to decrease labour costs. With recent legislative changes, this has become the case for many companies in the U.S.

A second recommendation for specific information to present in a business case is the company's labour history. Does the company go through growth modes where it has struggled to find enough talent only to release this talent in the next economic downturn? If so, plot these historical events on the same chart where you mapped out the revenue and labour expenses. If you can put a cost to these actions, and even provide an estimate of cost savings resulting from evening out the labour shortages and surpluses, this information is rather valuable.

Another piece of information which can be provided only requires the addition of headcount information. Take the historical revenue values and divide them by the historical headcount numbers to produce "revenue per FTE." An FTE is a "full time equivalent" worker. An increase in this value over time shows that, on average, each employee is producing more revenue for the company. That's not to say that each employee actually produces revenue but it is a measure of the company's efficiency. A decline in this value over time may be an indicator that the organization is "becoming fat." An improvement to this metric would be to use the net income value instead of revenue in order to work in the impact of expense trends. A further refinement could be to calculate the value by business unit if you have enough information to allocate revenue, expenses and headcount across the units. If any of the units have become less efficient over time, you may wish to drop any automatic headcount replacement policies that you have in place and challenge the business unit to alter its processes for efficiency gains instead.

Your business case should also contain a list of benefits to be gained from workforce planning. I have stated quite a few benefits throughout this book but one that people sometimes miss is the benefit you can gain from the very first step of the strategic workforce planning framework. Recalling that the first step is to determine the "roles of interest," why not communicate to your leadership that this list can be used to prioritize recruitment efforts? "Roles of interest" will be filled first. If your company has an automated employee requisition team, this would require IT programming changes. If your company competes for IT resources internally, getting these changes implemented becomes a much larger challenge.

Ensure that your business case outlines all of the peripheral benefits of workforce planning. As previously mentioned, scenario models can be used to model headcount. These headcount values can be used for training predictions, IT budgets, IT resource planning, uniform budgeting (if your employees are uniformed), real estate, retirement benefits, etc. Provide specific examples for your company in your business case to demonstrate that HR is not the only area which would benefit from strategic workforce planning efforts. This assists HR in being viewed as a true business partner.

My final piece of advice is to order your business case justifications such that the largest impact items are presented first. This will get the attention of your audience. Second, if you have some members of leadership who can't make it past the first slide before asking a long series of questions, at least you will have shown them your best first! You may find the opportunity to present some of the other material in response to the questions that are posed.

Challenges to Successful Implementation

Quite a few companies have been on the strategic workforce planning implementation journey for several years. That's not to say that strategic workforce planning is new but it has experienced a renewed focus since the downturn of the 2008 market when companies found they could not flex their workforce down fast enough in a strategic way. Many lost a substantial amount of critical talent when the only action they could take quickly was to execute a mass layoff. Without the assessment of critical roles in place, companies did not have the time to assess which roles were strategic and therefore should be out of scope during a layoff.

Having compared practices with many of these companies, every single one has experienced their own challenges. Some challenges we all have in common and some are unique. The following is a presentation of some of the more common challenges, keeping in mind that many companies start by "selling the business case."

In the previous section, we addressed the need to ensure that the business case was specific to your own company and not a general argument for strategic workforce planning. Even with a well-prepared business case, you may still fail to get the support of leadership.

The following section presents information and advice for strategic workforce planning leaders on how to move forward with these challenges.

Culture

Culture has a huge impact on the successful implementation of workforce planning. Given that the first step most people take is to sell the business case to gain support for the strategic workforce planning process, you would benefit from an open-minded, progressive leadership. If they are not progressive and have perhaps grown stale in the position, then they have probably seen business cases for a variety of initiatives presented to them for years. The challenge in this case is to convince the leadership that your business case is so much more important to the future of the company than all the rest of the initiatives they are seeing.

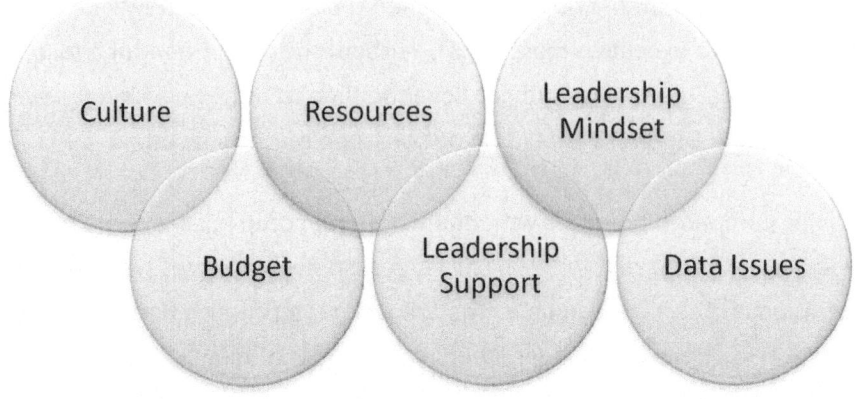

Figure 18: Challenges to Successful Implementation

If you don't manage to sell the business case for strategic workforce planning, refer to the section of this book entitled, *When Selling the Concept Just Didn't Work* for some guidance on how you can proceed.

Budget & Human Resources

You may very well find yourself in the situation where your leadership is sold on the concept, but cannot back it financially. Most companies who have succeeded in selling the concept and have obtained the financial backing have set up a central group to run the workforce planning process.

An additional trend in this area is that some companies have hired only the lead in charge of workforce planning and it is that lead's first goal to determine how much funding is needed to build the capabilities (personnel, software, data services etc.).

A second challenge in the area of resources is the readiness of HR to guide the discussions on "roles of interest," to perform the analysis of the current state and to model the future state. If you do not currently have the capabilities inside HR to forecast headcount, you will need to seek other resources in either your finance team or a strategy team if one exists.

Leadership Support

Suppose the top leadership supports and funds the concept of workforce planning. To be successful, you now need to work with the head of each division or sub-organization to be successful. In the companies with which I am most familiar, the people with whom one must work are one level below the people who supported and funded the concept. It is now possible that not all of this level "wishes to play." Don't get too concerned over this as I have found that those with the most urgent needs on the workforce front will be more than happy to accept whatever help they can get to solve their problems. You'll have their support without even having to show them a business case!

Ensure that you remain focused on the business strategy and the critical roles and don't let leaders distract you by having you solve all of their workforce problems. You have limited resources and should focus on solving the critical issues.

Leadership Mindset

The challenge in the leadership mindset is similar to some cultural challenges already presented, but this challenge specifically references how the leadership thinks. If the leaders who sit with HR to discuss "roles of interest" and scenario planning do not have the ability to envision the future, your scenario planning will consist of running "steady as she goes" plans. They may very well be able to look forward in terms of financial planning but it is far more difficult to envision skill sets and competencies needed in the future, especially if they don't exist in the market today. How many people envisioned needing computer programmers to program iPhone applications before the iPhone existed? We had no idea we would need "an app for that."

You may wonder how a company can survive this mindset. In a fast-moving technology industry, it can't, but in a mature industry with a product or service which is not rapidly changing, the impact of this thought challenge would be much smaller and there are always small pockets of forward thinkers in the organization to compensate.

The second mindset challenge is associated with a slight reversal of roles. Normally it would be the business unit leader or division leader who would tell HR how many people he needed to hire and into what roles. Now the leadership role is in the hands of the strategic workforce planning leader who guides the business leader through the process to determine what he / she needs and how many.

Giving up the leadership role may not be something the internal customer is willing to do. This is where it is very important to recognize and communicate that the role of HR is not to take over the leadership role, but rather to facilitate the process on behalf of the customer.

Additionally, when you approach the business unit or division leader with the concept of strategic workforce planning, it may be perceived as an HR activity solely for the benefit of HR. Again, selling the concept of HR as the facilitator for the purpose of meeting their workforce needs is the mindset you need to stress.

Data Issues

When you reach the point in the workforce planning process where you are trying to establish the current state and past trends, you have no chance of drawing any sound conclusions if your data is inaccurate. This is the classic "garbage in; garbage out" issue. This is why I believe that the person leading the workforce planning initiative has to be able to understand a certain amount of the IT world or at least be logical enough to determine the root cause of data inaccuracies.

You may also find yourself in a situation where some of the data you need for your scenario planning just doesn't exist in your company. In this case, you will need to determine if it's worth the cost of embarking on a journey of data system creation or whether you can simplify your scenario planning to eliminate the need for this information.

As an example of where some companies are in terms of HR data challenges, we'll look at Southern California Edison and Hitachi Data Systems. These are both very representative of the challenges most large companies face and the magnitude of effort and time required to implement a solution.

In a conference presentation given in 2012, John Vitali presented the state of Edison's workforce analytics as being primarily reporting. He indicated challenges associated with inconsistent data definitions, the need for pre-emptive actions, improved efficiencies and effectiveness and the need to minimize risk. He proposed a solution of awareness, available analytics for decision support and a more integrated approach. The company had a loss of data continuity and interpretation challenges. Vitali proposed a solution of establishing a super-user community in close partnership with IT and established an organized listing of internal clients, their needs and the technology needed to serve them. An additional action from Vitali which I recommend for all HR groups was to create a data dictionary for HR measures. A data dictionary is a document containing the names and official definitions of data fields used within an organization.

Similarly, Levent Arabaci from Hitachi Data Systems (Arabaci, 2012) presented his "journey to unleash the human potential." Like many companies operating in multiple countries, this company had no global employee records, no headcount reporting capabilities, no recruitment tracking systems, the inability to rank employees globally and many other challenges. To transform his HR data capabilities, Arabaci created a vision for HR and the business to align these efforts with the business objectives and to highlight the value in that alignment. To understand the full magnitude of this transformational journey, Arabaci presented a five year roadmap for Hitachi's HRIS.

The point of these examples is to demonstrate that depending on what information is missing in your HR systems and the availability of resources to assist you, the journey to put a system in place to start collecting the missing information may take a long time. Meanwhile, it would be wise to ensure that you have other activities which can show value to your leadership in the short term. This will help you sustain the level of leadership interest and support required to be successful with workforce planning.

Implementation Planning

Implementation planning for strategic workforce planning can be a daunting task. It is difficult to log all of the considerations that go into creating a successful plan.

- Who are the stakeholders?
- Where are they located?
- How will we establish relationships with them?
- How will we communicate with them?
- How often will we communicate with them?

Even the communication planning can be fairly extensive. Can in-person relationships be established with all of the stakeholders? Are they local employees or are they half-way around the globe? If they are out of the country, what is the culture around relationship forming? Will a conference call be sufficient or does the first meeting need to be face-to-face before trust is established?

If you succeed in forming the right relationships, the next step is to convince the stakeholders that they "need what you are selling." Andrew Jacobus from Hunt Consolidated Inc. (Jacobus, 2012) made a good point on this topic at a recent conference when he recognized that needs and wants of user groups vary and that a key to success is to "identify different user groups and address potential points of resistance." Understanding each of his customers and how each group used HR information allowed him to "develop audience-specific strategies."

Beyond relationships and communications, you need to establish data and technology plans, namely,

- assess current data sources,
- evaluate effectiveness of existing metrics, and
- assess available internal and external technology.

In the previous section, both Edison and Hitachi demonstrated the magnitude of effort associated with a data and technology plan.

An additional planning aspect is centered around reporting. Based on what each internal customer needs, how will you report it? Who is responsible for report generation? Can this be automated? How often should this information be generated? How much can we standardize the information across our array of customers? How do we integrate this information with our communication plan? How will we handle and track issues related to this plan?

A special point made by Scott Pollak (Pollak, 2012) from PwC is that "executives don't know what they want etc." While this sounds somewhat humourous, when it comes to human capital reporting, it is often true. It is the role of the strategic workforce planning leader to guide these executives to the data solutions which allow them to make solid, data-driven decisions for their area of the business. I also agree with Pollak's assessment that a one-size fits all approach to strategic workforce planning isn't the way to go. While heading up workforce planning for a global company, the challenges in the North American locations are entirely different than the challenges faced elsewhere.

In terms of phasing your implementation, Nicholas Garbis (Garbis, 2011) from GE Energy presented a three level approach. The first level is very similar to the strategic workforce planning framework outlined near the beginning of this book in that it contains an assessment of the roles, supply, demand, gaps and action plans. His second level adds additional capabilities like cost modeling, multiple scenarios and assessment of external supply. The final level assesses the action plan options, adds competency modeling, ROI and risk assessment.

Levels of SWP Capabilities

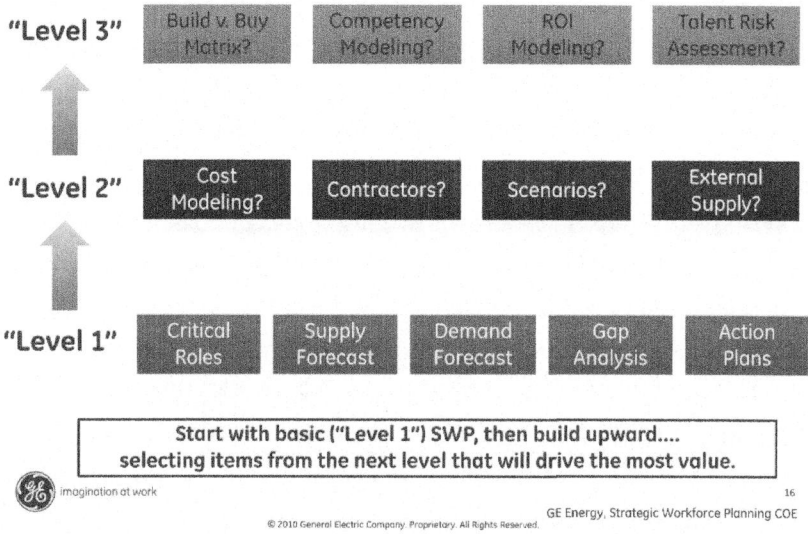

Figure 19: GE Energy Approach to Strategic Workforce Planning Implementation

My implementation approach, which was for a global, Fortune 100 company, has been fairly similar although the competency capabilities existed earlier in the implementation. The framework I have presented in this book contains all of the components that Garbis presents above, so if the reader wishes to implement that framework, the three phased plan of Garbis is an excellent planning resource. Start by assessing which components you have today or can get quickly. Define those to be your "Level 1" and grow from there.

A similar process has been used by Southern California Edison in collaboration with Vemo (Michael Manning, 2012) where a three year plan is suggested. Their basic structure is as follows:

79

1. Year 1: Focus on planning and asking "what."
2. Year 2: Focus on planning and analytical insights to ask "what" and "why."
3. Year 3: Advanced planning to answer "what," "why" and "how."

At this point, it might be a good idea to create a checklist of the implementation components you will need for your own company. What is in existence today that you can leverage to move ahead faster and show "quick wins?" How should you define your levels of capabilities to phase your implementation?

With the vast number of questions proposed in consideration for strategic workforce planning implementation, I am certain that this section has demonstrated the magnitude of planning required to implement strategic workforce planning in an organization. The effort requires a great deal of thought, discussion, planning and tracking.

When Selling the Concept Just Didn't Work

You did your research, you created a fabulous business plan, you communicated the plan to your management and then it didn't get approved. Perhaps the company can't afford the cost of implementing the entire plan. Perhaps your leadership has seen so many pie-in-sky business cases that these just don't have an impact anymore. Perhaps your leadership feels that the company has done so well for so long that they see no need for anything new. Whatever the reason may be, the question on the table is "now what do you do?"

My advice in this situation is to begin with what you can. Evaluate your plan to see which items are lower cost but will show immediate value. It has been my experience that having specific results to show which address a specific problem will yield a supporter for your effort. Focus on gaining these supporters through results rather than spending your time trying to convince them with business case documents.

It has also been my experience that people unfamiliar with workforce planning just can't envision what it can do for them. This is another reason why specific workforce examples work so well. After several of these, you will find that people will start to come to you with requests. After doing a few examples in two countries, I began to get enquiries from other global locations within the company.

If you have absolutely no budget for this effort, focus on strategic workforce efforts using existing data systems which would perhaps yield cost savings. Of course, ensure that the data system you use is reliable enough to conduct a valid workforce planning analysis. Perhaps the realization of cost savings on one activity can be applied toward a workforce planning investment.

Measuring Success

For those companies that created entirely new departments to perform the strategic workforce planning function, how do you know that your investment in strategic workforce planning is working? For those that found the need to completely restructure the way HRIS (Human Resource Information Systems) work in order to support workforce planning efforts, how do you demonstrate the value of that investment to your leadership? Do you put metrics in place? What do you measure?

A great deal of discussion has taken place on this topic but after benchmarking with other companies, I am not under the impression that many have put in place a way to measure the success of their strategic workforce planning efforts...and that's ok. For where most people are in the implementation journey, it is far more important to direct your resources toward solving the company's issues than worrying about which metrics should be assigned to workforce planning. It is my opinion that the problems being addressed by workforce planning are so wide in scope that a series of metrics to monitor the success would vary substantially from one company to the next.

For example, if one of your workforce planning efforts is to address a shortage of specialized engineers, then you may consider a "time to hire" or "length of time vacant" measurement to see if your efforts are yielding results. This metric would be specific to the "specialized engineer" job role which would have been identified in Step 1 of our workforce planning framework.

Using our IT programmer example from earlier in the book, suppose that the action plan you selected was to retain the redundant programmers and train them in the new programming languages your company needs. In this case, your metrics would be centered around training and measuring the competency development of the employees in this role.

As you can see, the metrics desired can be quite varied as they must relate to the specific problem you are trying to solve. Problem resolution and workforce solutions are, after all, the value the workforce planning group is providing.

If you do wish to head down the path of providing an overall metric, PcW Saratoga (Pollak, 2012) has proposed a metric called ROWI defined as,

$$ROWI = Unit\ Cost\ /\ Productivity.$$

Unit cost is the labour investment per employee (or FTE). While this looks fairly straight forward, trying to assess that value can get quite complex and some of the information required may not be obtainable. This gets even more complex when you are operating in hundreds of countries. What components do you include? Does your accounting system lend itself to providing enough detail to get the necessary values? Do you even have access to the accounting system? The effort required to establish a value is often not worth it, just to produce this metric. I favour the previous metrics which are directly related to the problems at hand and far easier to obtain.

The second issue with the ROWI metric is determining what to use as a productivity measure. While Pollak demonstrates this metric with revenue as the productivity measure, net income would be better otherwise the entire impact of expenses is ignored. Employees are responsible for keeping expenses in line with revenue. However, if the company is losing money, the net income is a negative value and not of much use in this calculation. While this concept would provide an overall metric for the effectiveness of workforce planning, there would be so many factors affecting this metric that trying to assess the drivers behind any change would take a lot of effort and yield little value.

The final issue with this metric is that rarely does HR have access to financial information on a real-time basis especially if the company is publically traded. This makes the ROWI very much a lagging measurement whereas metrics like vacancy rates, training measurements etc. are more likely to be close to real-time and accessible from within HR.

I4cp, in their strategic workforce planning playbook, outlines the top ten metrics organizations use to gauge workforce planning effectiveness.

1. Reductions in identified workforce gaps
2. Number of open positions or vacancies
3. Decrease in number of vacancies
4. Opinions of managers
5. Critical role vacancies
6. Opinions of employees
7. Number of internal succession candidates
8. Improvements in succession pipelines
9. Headcount
10. Cost savings in replacement costs

I like these better than the ROWI concept with the exception of the opinion metrics. What is missing here is that the metrics need to be restricted to the "roles of interest" which were established in Step 1 of the strategic workforce planning framework. Those are the roles to which the workforce planning group is dedicated so including roles outside of the scope of this group make the measurements inaccurate and put you more in a workforce analytics reporting mode than a strategic mode.

As you can see, a lot of thought needs to be dedicated to measuring success of workforce planning efforts. Personally, I prefer a tool which documents the problems, solutions and measurements in one place. Below is an example of this tool. It can be used to document multiple roles or multiple action plans on one role. I will use the previous IT programmer role for this example.

To explain the thought process behind these metrics, in Year 1 where a shortage of IT programmers will occur, the company does not have enough internal talent to meet their needs. They have decided to recruit from the external market whether that be existing experienced programmers or recruitment of new graduates from universities.

Role of Interest	Challenge	Action Plan	Measurement
IT Programmer	Shortage in Year 1 of the 5 year plan	Recruit from the external market.	Number of vacancies, time to fill, performance score after 6 months and 1 year.
IT Programmer	Surplus in Year 2	Talent development for new skill set.	Percentage of required training classes completed, competency evaluation scores, number awaiting transition, performance score after 6 months and 1 year.

To measure the success of this initiative in solving the problem of a shortage, the company can track the number of vacancies and the length of time it takes to fill these positions. Of course, people behave according to the metrics that guide them, so there is a risk that the recruitment team, in an effort to fill the positions quickly, will be tempted to let the quality of the hired candidates drop. The performance score after six months was selected as a metric to measure the quality of hire. Some companies prefer a measurement related to which school the candidate attended, the number of degrees etc.

There is another series of metrics which can be implemented on the scenario planning step of the workforce planning framework and those are related to accuracy. Previously, it was presented that scenario planning could include both headcount numbers and competency planning. When looking at headcount modeling, you could implement some of the following metrics in support of the value the program is providing. Accurate data on these projections can add to the business case in continuing the strategic workforce planning efforts.

- accuracy of retirement projections,
- accuracy of non-retirement termination projections, and
- accuracy of internal movement projections.

Like many aspects of the workforce planning initiative, selecting the right metrics is not a one size fits all list. For the individual efforts, I maintain that the metrics addressing the problem you are trying to solve are your best choice since that ensures the measurement is as closely tied to value as possible. I also favour the accuracy measurements above since the scenario plans are an input into the gap assessments. Inaccuracies in the forecast lead to inaccuracies in the gap assessments. Substantial inaccuracies lead to unpleasant surprises.

Roles and Responsibilities

If you have ever attended a conference on strategic workforce planning and paid attention to the job titles of the workforce planning leaders, you will quickly discover that they are quite varied. This is indicative not only of the variations of job titles within industries but also the variations in structures within organizations for this specialized function.

The majority of companies with which I have spoken have chosen a centralized approach, where the workforce planning activities are performed for the entire organization. In about 80% of these companies, the central group resides within Human Resources while the remainder reside in a centralized strategy group.

The advantage of a centralized group is that the expertise and specialized skills are housed in one location and it is easier to maintain consistent approaches and processes for this function. Many organizations already had a central HR analytics or survey team so a fairly easy solution was to grow these groups and have them take on the responsibilities of implementing strategic workforce planning. For companies that operate in one or only a few countries, this approach can work; for global companies operating in many countries, this is not optimal.

For large, global organizations, a regional approach is recommended. With such a large variation in workforce regulations across the globe, it would be impossible for a central workforce planning group to become educated on the limitations posed by these regulations. A centralized group may propose workforce solutions for a specific country, only to discover that local laws prevent implementation of that solution. That said, it is recommended that there be at least one workforce planning lead in a centralized location (or a small team if appropriate) to coordinate these global activities and to ensure that best practices in implementing the workforce planning framework are shared. This also ensures consistent processes across the regions, as much as local conditions will allow.

The final option for structuring workforce planning is to have a completely decentralized approach where each individual manager or business partner is responsible for his / her own workforce planning activities. For large companies, I do not recommend this approach because there is no one accountable for ensuring a consistent approach for workforce planning. From previous chapters, we have already seen that the workforce planning framework varies substantially from company to company depending on the internal structure of HR and strategy development groups. Under decentralization, there is no one responsible for educating business partners on workforce planning frameworks, tools and processes. The end result would be an inconsistent approach across the company.

However, for smaller companies, I can see a decentralized approach working under certain conditions. If a company is small enough that communication across functional lines is effective, then this company could rely on an external consultant to come in to educate the business partners and guide them through a consistent approach. With a small enough cross-functional leadership team, this same team could serve as both the strategy development team and the workforce planning team, especially since one function is so entwined with the functions and timing of the other.

Regardless of which structure a company selects, there are some common positions which will exist. For all three structure types, there is a strategic workforce planning lead. The only difference will occur in the decentralized structure if your workforce lead is an external consultant.

So, what are the responsibilities of the workforce planning lead? This lead provides the overall guidance for this strategic initiative. Whether an internal lead or an external consultant, this person educates the leadership on the best approach to implementing workforce planning activities.

This lead is responsible for communicating the established processes and tools for each of the workforce planning framework steps. He / she works with senior leadership to recommend workforce strategy and direction. If the company is large enough to have an economist, this lead also interacts with the economist to gain awareness of likely futures which will impact the workforce planning scenario building step.

If this lead has a centralized group in Human Resources and the company also has a centralized group for strategic planning (separate from the company's overall leadership), then the workforce planning lead interacts with the head of this strategic planning group on initiatives which combine operational and workforce planning.

The lead further aligns the workforce planning efforts with existing HR functions (succession planning, recruitment, talent management, training, etc.) as these individuals or groups (and others) are involved in setting action plans as a result of strategic workforce planning studies.

For global companies, the lead coordinates across country lines and is aware of the workforce challenges in all international regions in which the company operates. He / she leverages this awareness to prioritize workforce planning tool development and distribution of these tools to international locations.

The lead also directs the following activities and coordinates with other appropriate functional areas to:

- assess the available technology for workforce planning and its data needs (often in coordination with IT experts),
- conduct research and provide information on both internal and external workforce trends,
- align with talent management teams to provide insight into workforce trends requiring their attention,
- manage the workforce planning budget,
- evaluate and develop members of the strategic workforce planning team where one exists,
- provide training on the use of strategic workforce planning tools, and
- externally benchmark workforce planning practices with other organizations.

As mentioned previously, for most companies, the approach to implementing strategic workforce planning has been to form a group or expand the responsibilities of an existing group. Where these groups exist, the responsibilities of these team members will vary because the skill sets needed to perform all workforce planning responsibilities is quite broad. The role of these individuals can be to:

- define data needs including assessing commercial software,
- construct custom workforce planning tools,
- conduct research on workforce trends,
- facilitate meetings with business partners and other stakeholders,
- educate personnel on processes established as workforce planning standards within the company, and
- attend classes and conferences to remain current on workforce planning topics and to communicate this information back to the team and team lead.

What types of individuals should you look for when filling both the lead position and the individual team members? If you have benchmarked with other companies already, you have probably found that individuals in these roles have come from an assortment of backgrounds. Backgrounds include but are not limited to mathematics, IT, finance, operations, business strategy and business planning. While varied, the common factor is that very few of these individuals have come up through the traditional human resources career path. They are analytical. Let's take a look at the leader first.

Many companies have tried to promote from within to ensure that the workforce planning leader has knowledge of their business, but often the personalities of the highly-detailed analytical mind do not translate well to a leadership role. The leader should certainly have a background in a numerical discipline. This will prepare him / her for understanding the work performed by the analysts. However, the leader should not have spent their entire career in one functional area. Experience in multiple functional areas will better prepare the workforce planning leader to view key business problems from several points of view. Possessing a broad experience will prepare the leader for the compromises in solutions which inevitably occur. I would also recommend that the leader have either a business degree or equivalent work experience in order to understand how workforce planning impacts the bottom line and the need to produce a return on the company's investment in workforce planning.

Further, the leader needs to be interested in learning about technology. Part of this leadership function is to assess the IT technologies and investigate which technologies work best to solve the data structure, access and quality needs for workforce planning. A leader who has no interest in learning about databases or analyzing the "buy versus build" decision for workforce planning tools may find himself / herself making riskier decisions.

Near the top of the list, the lead must have the ability to form relationships inside and outside of the organization. Most business problems require that data be gathered from several functional areas and that a discussion be held with a cross-functional team. Without these relationships, moving workforce planning activities forward is far more challenging.

The final skill needed is leadership. Combining the above skills in such a way as to provide a vision of the road ahead to both the workforce planning team members and the company leadership will keep everyone motivated in this initiative. Implementing successful strategic workforce planning is a journey of several years so the team lead needs to keep everyone pointed in the same direction long enough to demonstrate strategic benefits from these activities. Many initiatives get off to a great start but the interest fades when value cannot be demonstrated quickly. Find some business problems which can be solved quickly using workforce planning techniques in order to demonstrate value as soon as possible.

Now let's take a look at some of the team members within a typical workforce planning group. First, we have need of some highly analytical employees. For the most part, people with analytical skill sets are very detail-oriented but somewhat introverted. For this reason, you will likely have some analytical personnel who perform the core analyses (and are very happy to do so) and a few that are "business savvy" enough to facilitate discussions with your business partners. Although harder to locate in the workforce, an individual with analytical skills, strong project management skills and great communication skills is worth their weight in gold. Without these individuals, far too many discussions will need to be facilitated by the workforce planning team lead.

I recommend screening your candidates carefully when hiring analytical employees. In addition to the considerations above, some analysts can run reports on data but do not have the ability to interpret the information. Some can tell you how the data is trending, but not tell you how that relates to the business. The employees you should hire are the ones who understand how the analytics translate into recommendations for action plans.

Depending on the extent to which you must evolve your data availability and data quality, you may need team members specialized in IT subjects. It is recommended that these individuals have superior project management skills. Additionally, they should be able to translate business needs from non-technical team members into technical terms needed to solidify requirements for IT personnel.

Occasionally, you can locate an individual who has knowledge of data analytics and IT structures which is quite valuable, but it should be noted that these skill sets are quite different. One *defines* how data will be structured and stored; the other is a *user* of the data and doesn't necessarily possess knowledge of the IT structures behind it.

Workforce Planning's Connection to HR Activities

"How does talent management relate to strategic workforce planning?" This is a popular question I am asked, so I felt the need to address it in its own section. At the same time, I will also illustrate the connection to other HR activities. Recall our definition of strategic workforce planning and the framework I am using in this book.

Strategic workforce planning is proactively planning to provide:

- the right number of people,
- with the right skill sets,
- in the right location,
- at the right time,
- at the right cost

to ensure successful completion of business objectives. Recall also that in some definitions you may see the first two bullets captured as "the right people" but I prefer to clarify that the right people actually means the right number with the right skills.

Strategic workforce planning activities determine the roles which require a greater focus in human resource groups and some groups outside of HR (IT, capacity planning, sourcing, etc.). The analyses required to forecast the needs of the company and the future gaps within these roles is also a workforce planning activity.

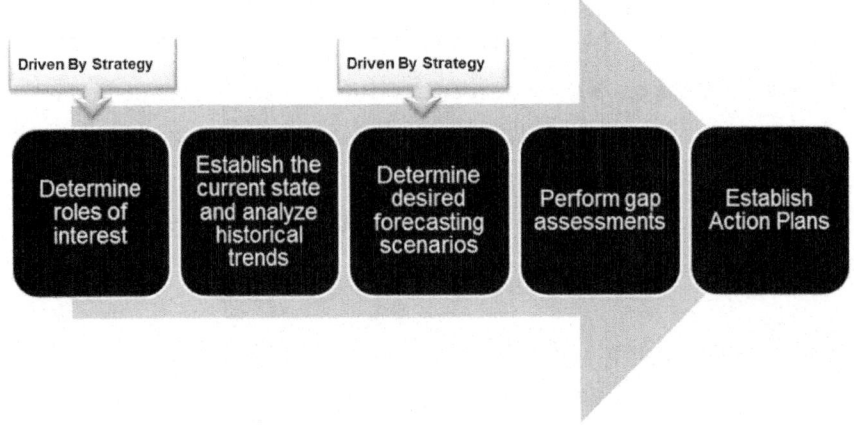

Figure 20: Author's Strategic Workforce Planning Framework

Where talent management and other HR areas come into play are in establishing the action plans in the final stage of the workforce planning activities. That's not to say that the strategic workforce planning team should operate in isolation and then pass the results on to the talent management team to implement. The talent management team (or individual) should be closely tied to the workforce planning team throughout the entire process.

The same recommendation is provided in relation to other human resource areas. Since the recommended action plans could be related to competency development, succession planning, recruitment, HR budgeting, organizational effectiveness, HR communications, performance management, rewards, training, engagement, retention, etc., representatives from these areas should be involved in multiple steps of the workforce planning framework. You may not need everyone in every step of the process but as your workforce planning processes evolve, you will be better able to judge which groups need to be involved in each step. Allow for flexibility since each workforce problem addressed will have differing solutions and involve different groups.

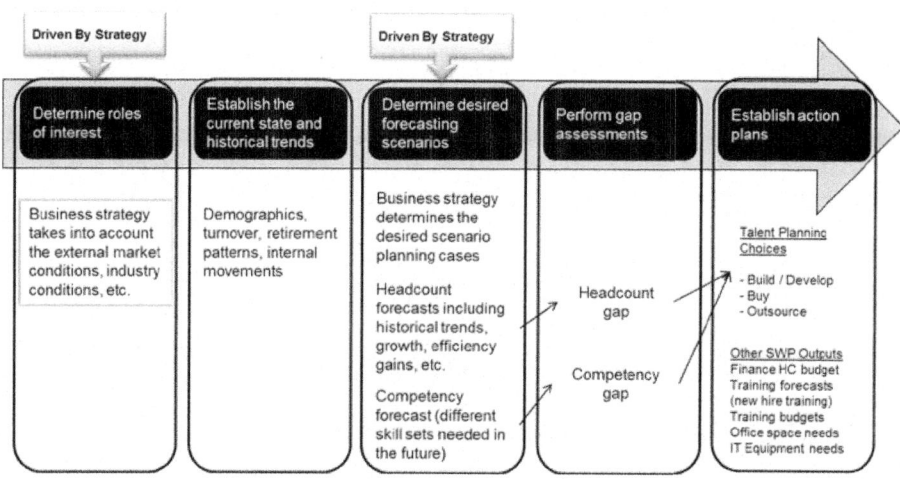

Figure 21: Details of Strategic Workforce Planning Framework

I have shown some of the possible activities in each of the workforce planning framework steps in the figure above (Figure 21: Details of Strategic Workforce Planning Framework). In the interest of space, it should be noted that this image is not showing a complete list of all possible activities.

4. Baby Boomers and the Risk to Your Leadership

By now, virtually everyone attached to strategic workforce planning has heard all about the baby boomer retirement wave and the concern companies have in replacing these workers.

In Canada, the birth rate per woman declined after the boom and in 2004, Canada reported its lowest birth rate since 1921 (Statistics Canada, p. 2012). The rate has increased in the years since but remains below the replacement rate to maintain the population.

In the U.S., the trend was very similar. The birth rate declined after the boom, had a peak in 1990 of 16.7 per 1,000 people followed by a 12 year decline. By 2002, the rate was down to 13.9. Seven years later, in the most recently reported data of 2009, the rate was 13.8.

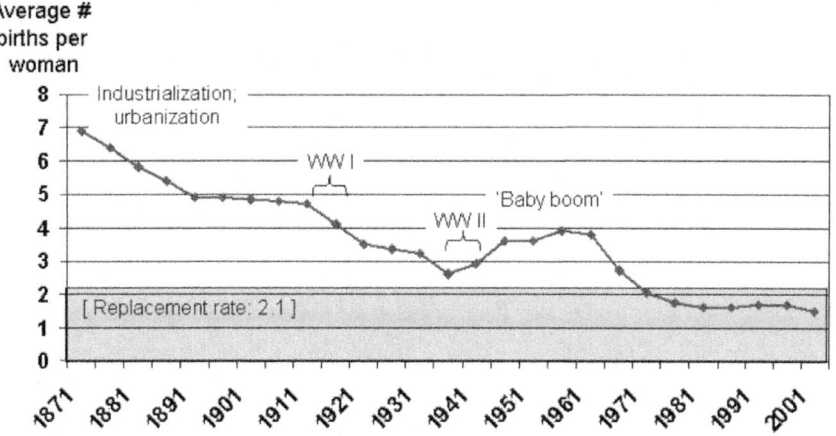

Figure 22: Canada - Historical Birth Rates

Japan's birth rates are even more concerning and have dropped from 9.9 per 1,000 people in the year 2000 down to 7.3 in 2011. The rates remain well below a level required to maintain the population and low immigration rates don't sufficiently offset this.

European trends vary by country but with the slowing economy, these countries are not attracting enough immigrants to maintain their population stability. Even one of the wealthiest countries, Germany, reported declining births in recent years.

The common theme throughout these examples is that the aging portion of the population is increasing. We hear repeatedly that there are not enough younger people coming up behind the boomers. This is only an issue because all of these countries have social programs in place to provide benefits for those who have retired. The retired population collects from the social programs, while the younger population pays into the social programs during their working years. These two populations are now out of balance.

So, what do the baby boomers have to do with the risk to your leadership? For companies that have been around for decades, chances are that baby boomers are a significant portion of the leadership. There is a good chance that these leaders will begin retiring in larger numbers than they have historically. There are certainly variations to retirement ages depending on historical events and economic conditions, but in general there will be an increase in coming years.

Many consultants on this topic would have you believe that half of your leadership will retire in the next five years and that you have a huge risk to the continuity of your leadership. My first thoughts upon hearing this were:

- you don't know my leadership,
- you don't know my data, and
- you don't know my company.

So before you panic, I will demonstrate in the following pages how I assessed the leadership risk of a global organization and proved that the risk to the continuity of the leadership was incredibly small. You may wish to try the same type of analysis on your leadership. This example will be somewhat simplified from the real analysis and the numbers changed to protect the privacy of the company.

This company operates in, say, three global regions. Let's consider the leadership to consist of all employees at or above the Vice President level. I first took a look at the historical turnover data to see what the trends were for these employees. Most had been with the company for a very long time and terminations were almost always by retirement. Additionally, the company is in a mature state so growth rates are not large.

These two pieces of information together tell me that the volume of leadership positions will be fairly constant for the next few years and that "demand" for these positions is primarily created through retirements.

Next, I took a look at the typical retirement ages for each of these three regions to see when I could expect vacancies to occur. As an aside, consultants speaking in generalities are basing their retirement statements on when someone is *eligible* to retire. In my case, I care far more about when they *actually* retire because there is a substantial enough difference in eligible versus actual to provide the company with several more years of planning time if they need it.

Using the above information, I flagged each leadership position with a risk level based on their age. If they were above the typical retirement age for their region, they were red; if they were within five years of it, they were yellow; otherwise they were green. This type of mapping made it very clear that half of our leadership was <u>not</u> likely to retire in the next few years.

The assessment did not stop there. Looking at the succession planning data collected in all of the regions, I flagged a risk level to the continuity of a position in the event that it became vacant. Without providing the exact definition, I'll say that positions that had ample supply ready were flagged as green; positions that had some but not enough to meet our definition of green were labeled yellow; positions that had no one ready were flagged as red.

Now we get a bit more sophisticated. The total risk of continuity for a position was an alignment of the risk level of vacancy combined with the risk level of the supply...and the result? There is very little risk to the continuity of the leadership, and now we have a very visual tool to focus our efforts on the small number of positions requiring attention. It also identified areas of the organization where there was a surplus of supply (shown as orange) which could be used for potential growth positions.

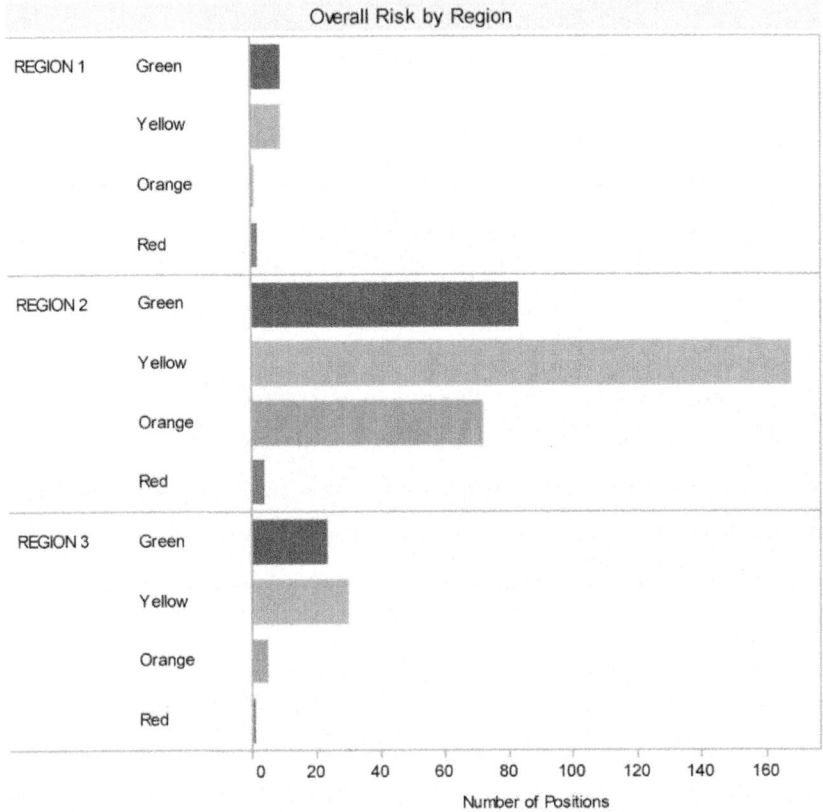

Figure 23: Excerpt of possible leadership risk visualizations

If you review this example and are thinking about how to make this work for a region which is growing, all you have to do is add the growth positions for the next few years to your list and assess your supply against both the existing and soon-to-be-created positions.

As a final option, if an area of your company is actually shrinking, these retirement projections and projections of non-retirement terminations can provide you with a natural attrition method of decreasing your employee base in lieu of downsizing.

At this point, I would like to provide a bit of advice so you don't fall into the trap that I have seen so many follow. Don't assume that data on the population as a whole will be true for your own company. Analyze your own data to see if it's true for you. As you can see from the previous example, broad generalizations about the baby boomer population were not true for this company. Instruct your people to stop making decisions on what they *think* is true and make decisions on what they *know* is true.

As a final comment, while this example was conducted on a leadership segment of roles, the process works for any selected role segment.

5. Concluding Remarks

There is no mistaking the value of strategic workforce planning as it aims to mitigate the workforce risk in an uncertain, global economy. There is also no mistaking the magnitude of effort required to fully implement a completely integrated workforce planning process. It is truly a journey of several years and a journey of insight.

The workforce planning evolution began years ago with headcount planning and slowly migrated into workforce analytics where internal trends became more evident. Modern day activities begin to focus on predictive capabilities, examining both internal and external trends and alignment to the business strategy.

I have endeavoured to provide readers of this book with a brief history of the workforce planning evolution and to provide a multitude of potential benefits which can be realized with strategic workforce planning.

The strategic framework presented in this book is one which can be implemented by any organization and I have provided a description of all five steps. With this framework, and the advice provided on staged implementation, the reader can embark on their own journey.

This book has presented a variety of approaches and tools to assist the reader in implementation and these approaches can be tailored to any organization.

Additionally, potential mathematical models and possible consideration factors have been shared and a description of the interaction between workforce planning and other areas of the organization has been presented.

Many of the top implementation challenges facing workforce planning leaders have been outlined and advice provided on how to attempt to overcome these challenges.

Additional advice has been provided on how to extract value from workforce planning long before a full implementation has been completed. Recommendations for aligning metrics to workforce planning problem solving have been given to measure specific value.

Further recommendations have been provided on the roles and responsibilities of workforce planning personnel in order to guide those currently hiring expertise into these groups.

The book concluded with a practical example on how to use workforce demographics, trends and succession planning information to assess the risk to critical positions within the organization.

Enjoy the journey...

Numerical Insights on the Web

Looking to find out more about Numerical Insights and what we can do for your company? We offer the following services:

- On-site corporate workshops to teach your HR team to use analytics and strategic workforce planning,
- Speaking engagements,
- Personalized consulting services on HR analytics and workforce planning, and
- Retainer agreements for business leaders looking to learn more about analytics.

You can find me on the web at **www.numericalinsights.com**. Our web site contains a sign-up newsletter list if you wish to be notified of future publications or information regarding analytics.

Twitter ID: @ninsights

Web Site: www.numericalinsights.com

LinkedIn: https://www.linkedin.com/in/numericalinsights

Appendix A: Tools and Templates

Step 1: Determine Roles of Interest

SWP Conversation Guideline for Determining "Roles of Interest"

What is a "role of interest?"

A role of interest is one which is connected to strategic execution and/or maintaining our competitive strengths, now and in the near future. These positions are flagged by Strategic Workforce Planning as those requiring prioritized attention in order to maintain a supply of "the right" talent.

Step 1: Role Identification

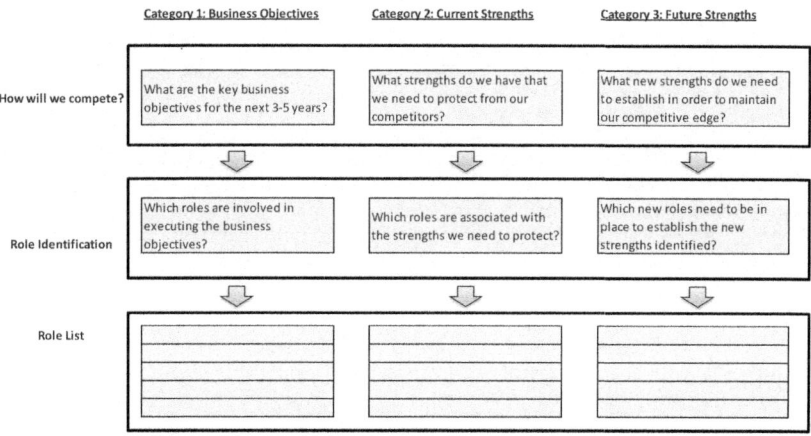

Step 2: Role Prioritization

Note: This step is performed on the list of roles identified above. This step can be optional if the list of roles above is fairly short.

1. Of the roles identified, which (if any) develop strategy?

2. Of the roles identified, where will a shortage of employees impact strategic execution the most?

3. Of the roles identified, where will a shortage of employees impact our competitive strengths the most?

4. Of the roles identified, where will a shortage of employees impact our financial performance the most?

Step 2: Establishing the Current State

Master List of Significant Events

This tool is designed to guide you through recording significant events in the company history which impact the projection methods of past trends.

Step 1: Enter a brief description of the past event.

Step 2: Record the date on which the event took place.

Step 3: Record the impacted roles.

Step 4: Record the impacted regions.

Past Event	Date	Impacted Roles	Impacted Region
Economic downturn	Nov. 2008	All hourly roles	USA
Outsourcing	Feb. 2010	Accounts payable roles	Canada, USA
Restructuring (Voluntary Packages)	Apr. 2011	IT, Sales	Germany

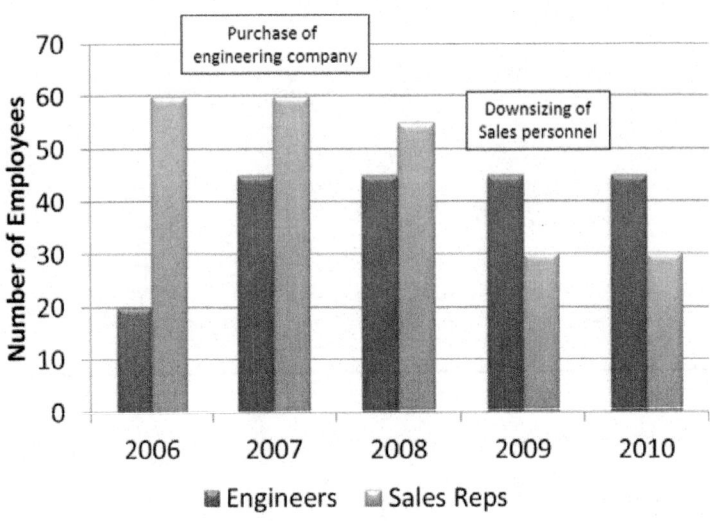

Step 3: Determine Desired Forecasting Scenarios

Scenario Development Tool

This tool is designed to guide you through developing a list of scenarios for each of your "roles of interest."

Step 1: From the list you developed in the "Determine Roles of Interest" step of the Strategic Workforce Planning framework, select one role to be the focus of this tool. The intent is to use this tool for each "role of interest."

Step 2: Conduct a meeting with internal customers related to this role and brainstorm the anticipated changes which may impact the future of this role.

Step 3: Record the resulting scenario plans needed to assess the impact of anticipated changes.

Role Segment:

Categories of Potential Changes Impacting this Role	Anticipated Changes Impacting This Role	Resulting Scenario Plans for Simulation
Business growth		
Competency changes		
Geographic considerations		
Technological changes		
Structural changes		
Business process changes		
Market changes		
Social changes		
Other		

Step 4: Perform Gap Assessments

Headcount Gap Assessment

Sample Workforce Forecasting Model Role: IT Programmers	Historical Data		Future Headcount				
	1 Year Ago	Today	Year 1	Year 2	Year 3	Year 4	Year 5
Total Headcount at start of Fiscal Year		147	149	180	160	145	145
Retirement Estimates							
Will Have Reached Retirement Age		30	35	42	44	49	55
Percentage Anticipated to Retire	4.8%	5.4%	5.1%	5.4%	5.6%	5.9%	6.1%
Total Estimated Retirements		8	8	10	9	9	9
Losses by Non-retirement Methods							
Estimated Reduction by Turnover		7	7	8	7	6	6
Estimated Reduction by Internal Moves		5	5	6	5	5	5
Total Non-retirement Losses		12	12	14	12	11	11
Total Losses During the Year		20	20	24	21	20	20
Headcount Needs for Significant Events							
New hires to program new systems		2	31				
Release of employees supporting old systems				(20)	(15)		
Total Recruitment Needs		22	51	4	6	20	20

Competency Gap Assessment

Strategic Objective	Skills Today	Skills Needed Tomorrow
Creation and Support of New IT Systems	Project Management	Project Management
	Internal Relationships	Internal Relationships
	Cobol, Fortran	C++, C#
	Time Management	Time management
		Process improvement

Environmental Scanning Reference

This tool is designed as a reference for the various types of internal and external environmental scanning activities.

Internal	External
Employee demographics	Political stability
Employee tenure	Industry growth / maturity
Career development opportunities	Inflation
Trends for retirements and non-retirement turnover	Exchange rates
Employee engagement	Tax laws
Financial constraints	Consumer demographics
	Technology changes

Appendix B: Other Publications by the Author

Tracey is the author of **HR Analytics: The What, Why and How**.

This book is not intended to teach mathematical techniques. It is intended for a non-mathematical audience.

This book is designed for those migrating out of reporting into HR analytics and for students looking to understand how their analytical talents fit into Human Resources.

This book will explain the levels of value on an HR Analytics road map and will provide practical advice on selecting metrics, designing dashboards and setting up an analytics problem.

A chapter is dedicated to simple examples to demonstrate how to use a business view to plan analytics projects.

The book examines the advantages and disadvantages of trying to build these capabilities in-house and will provide a realistic view of the challenges you will face as an analyst or leader.

The concept of building a linkage map to connect HR to the business is demonstrated.

Tracey is also the author of **The Best is Yet to Come: Expert Advice on Building the New HR.**

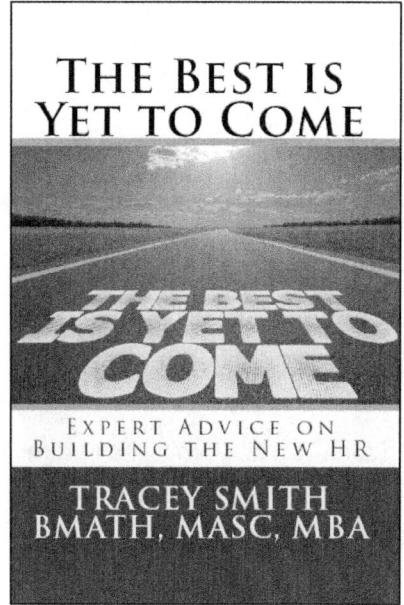

The Human Resource function is under pressure to migrate out of being a tactical function and into serving the business in a strategic role. Yet, year after year, most HR teams struggle to move forward. Why is that? This book is intended to help you understand the strategic journey on which HR finds itself today. Through research and interviews with expert leaders, this book outlines HR's past, the experiences of the present and the challenges of the future. Hear from today's leaders how they have succeeded in moving their HR functions forward. Experts weigh in from current and past leaders of TD Bank, FedEx, Johnson & Johnson, Press Ganey, Edison International, the State of Arizona, GP Strategies, Siemens, Merck, American Express and GE.

Shorter e-Books are also available on the following topics:

- Gender Gaps in the Workplace: Facts and Science
- The Strategy of Metrics & Key Performance Indicators

Bibliography

(2006). Conference Board.

Eyes Wide Open: Embracing Uncertainty Through Scenario Panning. (2009, July). Retrieved from Knowledge At Wharton: http://knowledge.wharton.upenn.edu/article.cfm?articleid=2298

Guide to Prioritizing Critical Employee Segments for Workplace Planning. (2010). *CLC Human Resources.*

Crucible Roles Business Case. (2011). CLC Human Resources.

(2012). Retrieved 08 05, 2012, from Shell Scenarios: See What the Future Might Look Like: http://www.shell.com/home/content/future_energy/scenarios/

(2012). *Metrics, Schmetrics.* i4cp Productivity Blog.

Arabaci, L. (2012). Transforming Human Resources.

Becker, B. E. (2009). *The Differentiated Workforce.* Harvard Business Press.

Capelli, P. (2008). *Talent on Demand: Managing Talent in an Age of Uncertainty.* Harvard Business School Press.

Fister, S. (2012). *SHRM Developing Metrics to Gauge Human Capital Assets.* Workforce.com.

Garbis, N. (2011). Strategic Workforce Planning at GE Energy.

Gross, J. (2008). *Workforce Planning Benchmark Study.* Hudson, Ohio: Top Grade Workforce Planning.

i4cp. (2012). *Strategic Workforce Planning Playbook.* i4cp.

Institute, H. C. (2010).

Jacobus, A. (2012). Driving a Strategic Talent Framework with Workforce Planning and Analytics.

Michael Manning, P. L. (2012). How to Successfully Launch Enterprise Workforce Planning.

Morrison, C. (2012). *Strategic Workforce Planning Practitioner Insights Report.*

Pollak, S. (2012). ROWI and Workforce Intellligence.

Ramstad, J. W. (2007). *Beyond HR: The New Science of Human Capital.* Boston, Massachusetts: Harvard Business School Press.

Roxburgh, C. (2009, November). *McKinsley Quarterly.* Retrieved from The Use and Abuse of Scenarios: https://www.mckinseyquarterly.com/Strategy/Strategy_in_Practice/The_use_and_abuse_of_scenarios_2463

Snell, S. (n.d.). *Mapping Human Capital Architecture.* Cornell University, School of Industrial and Labor Relations.

Statistics Canada. (n.d.). Retrieved from www.statcan.gc.ca

Vitali, J. (2012). Competitive Advantage through Workforce Planning & Analytics. *Financial Planning and Analysis.*

Printed in Great Britain
by Amazon

18299101R00071